Bedtime Stories Vol I

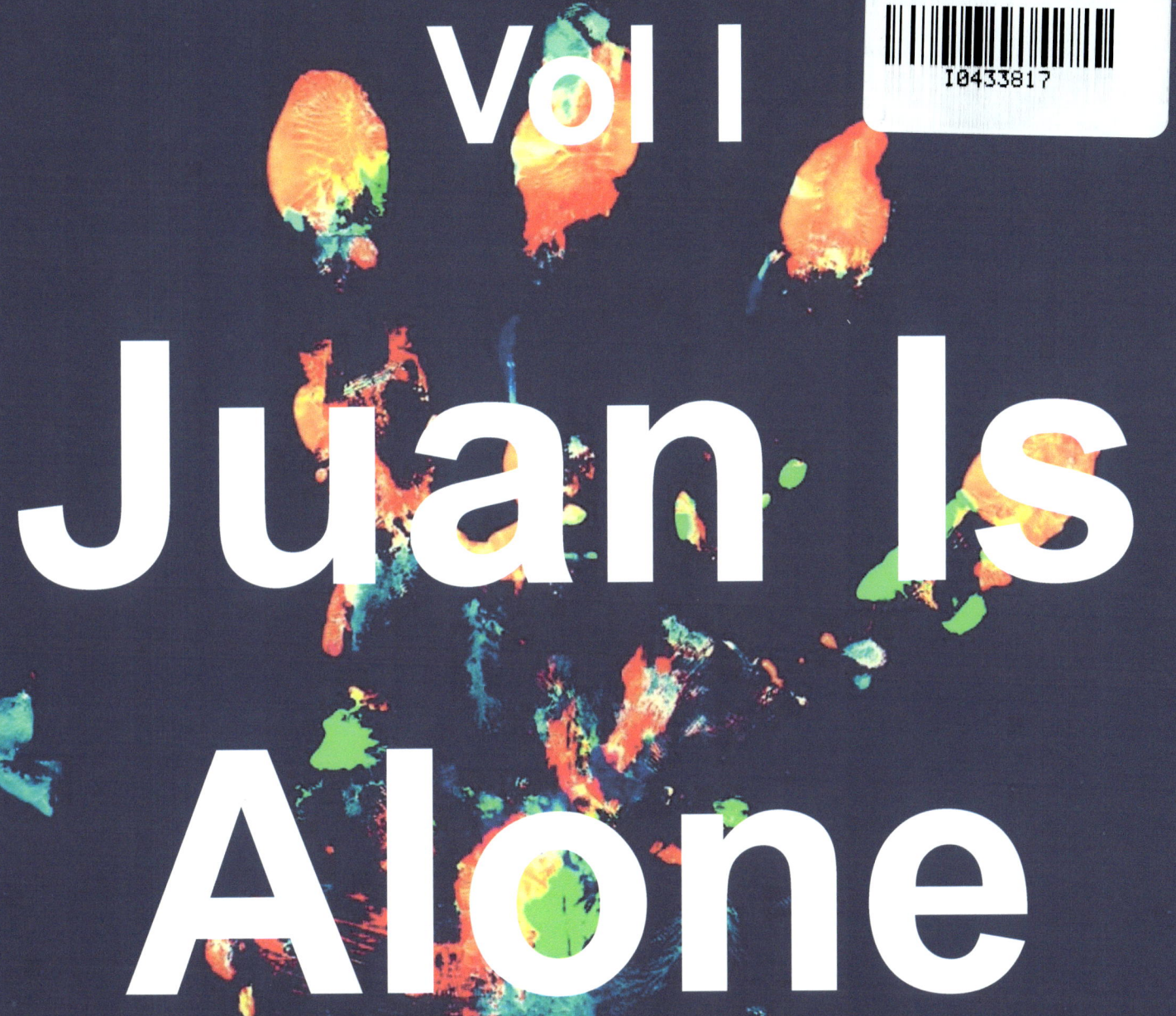

Juan Is Alone

Written By A Lonely Juan

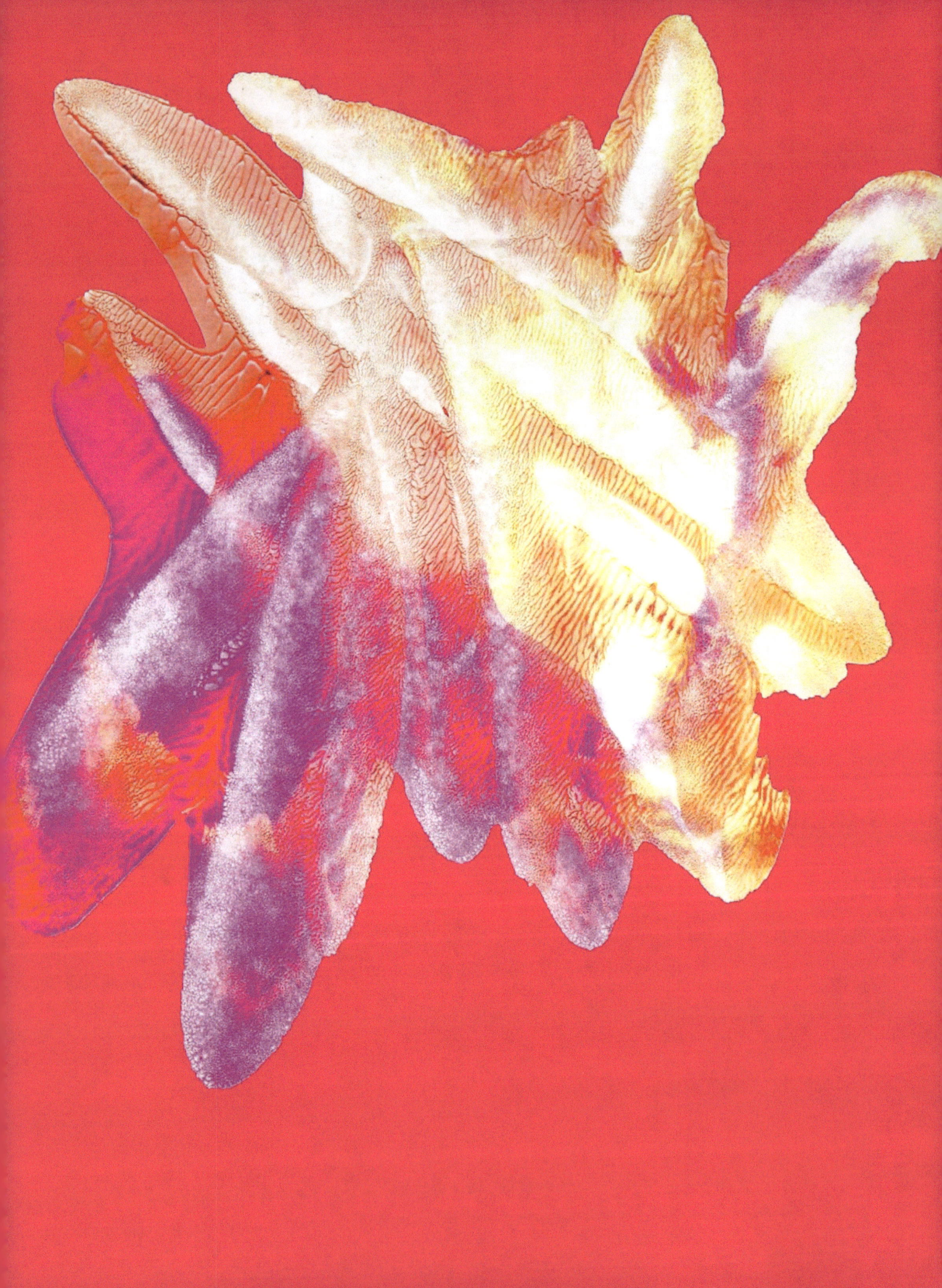

He's alone.
He's been known by many names.
In this story his name is Juan.

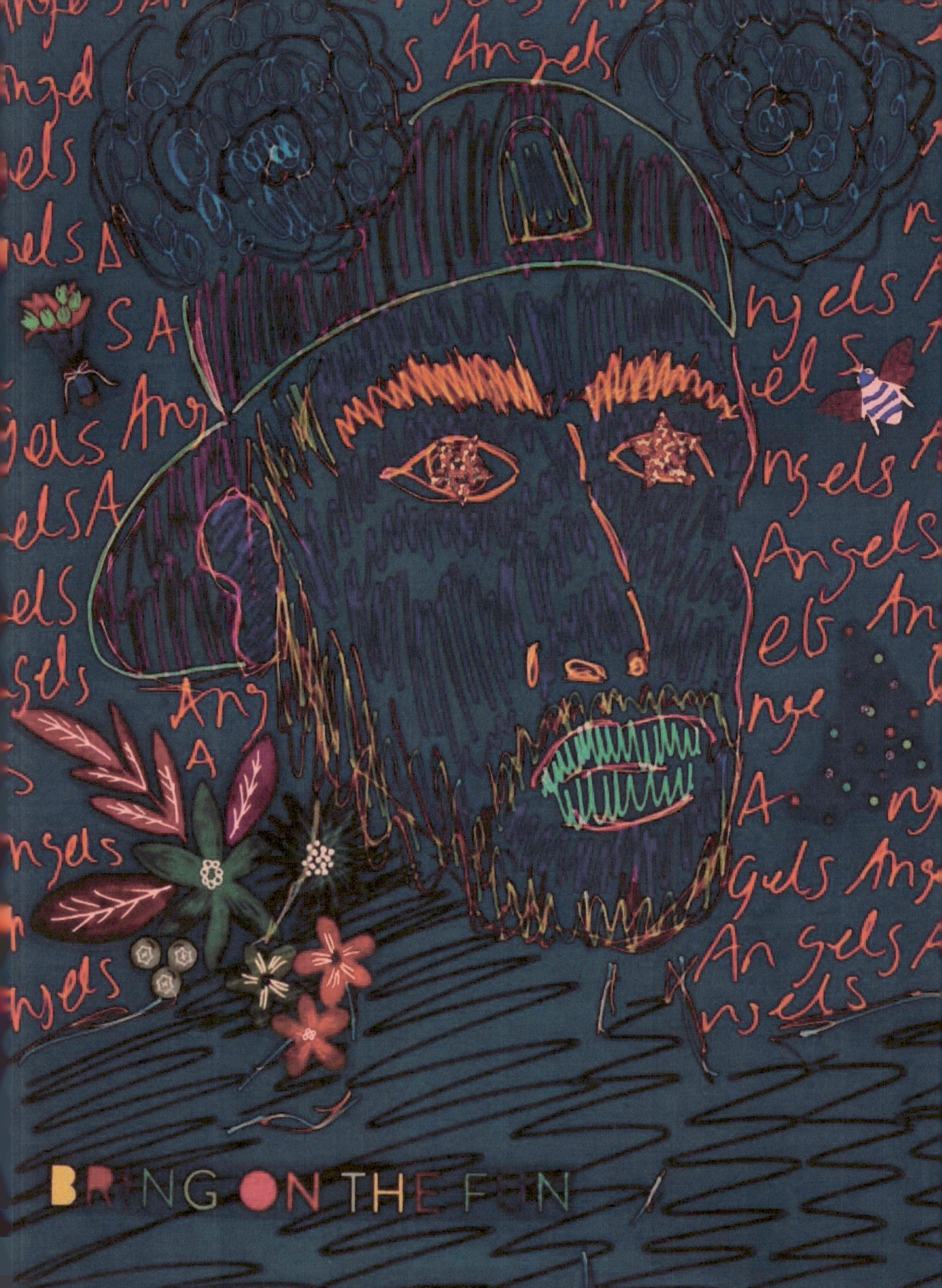

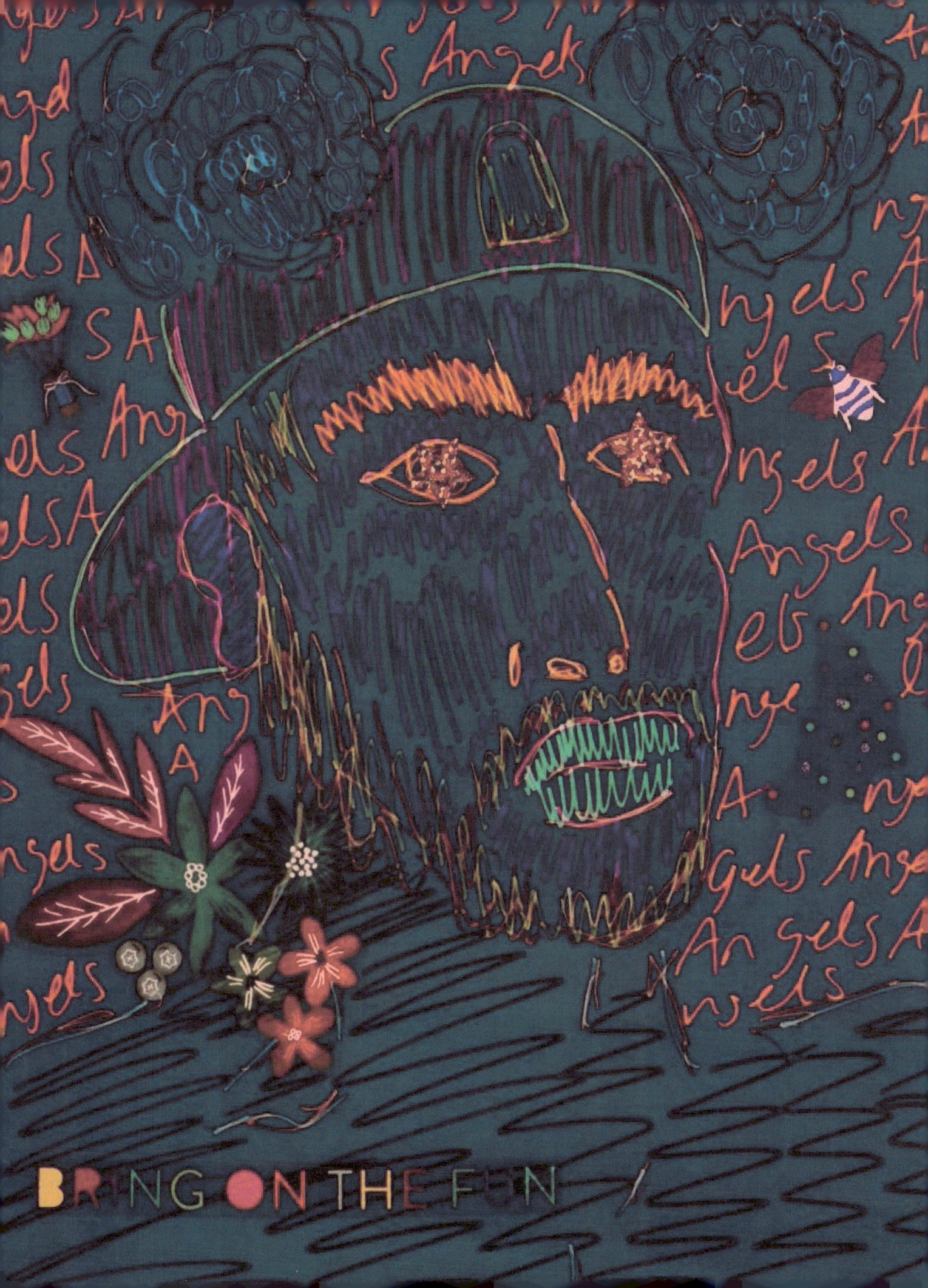

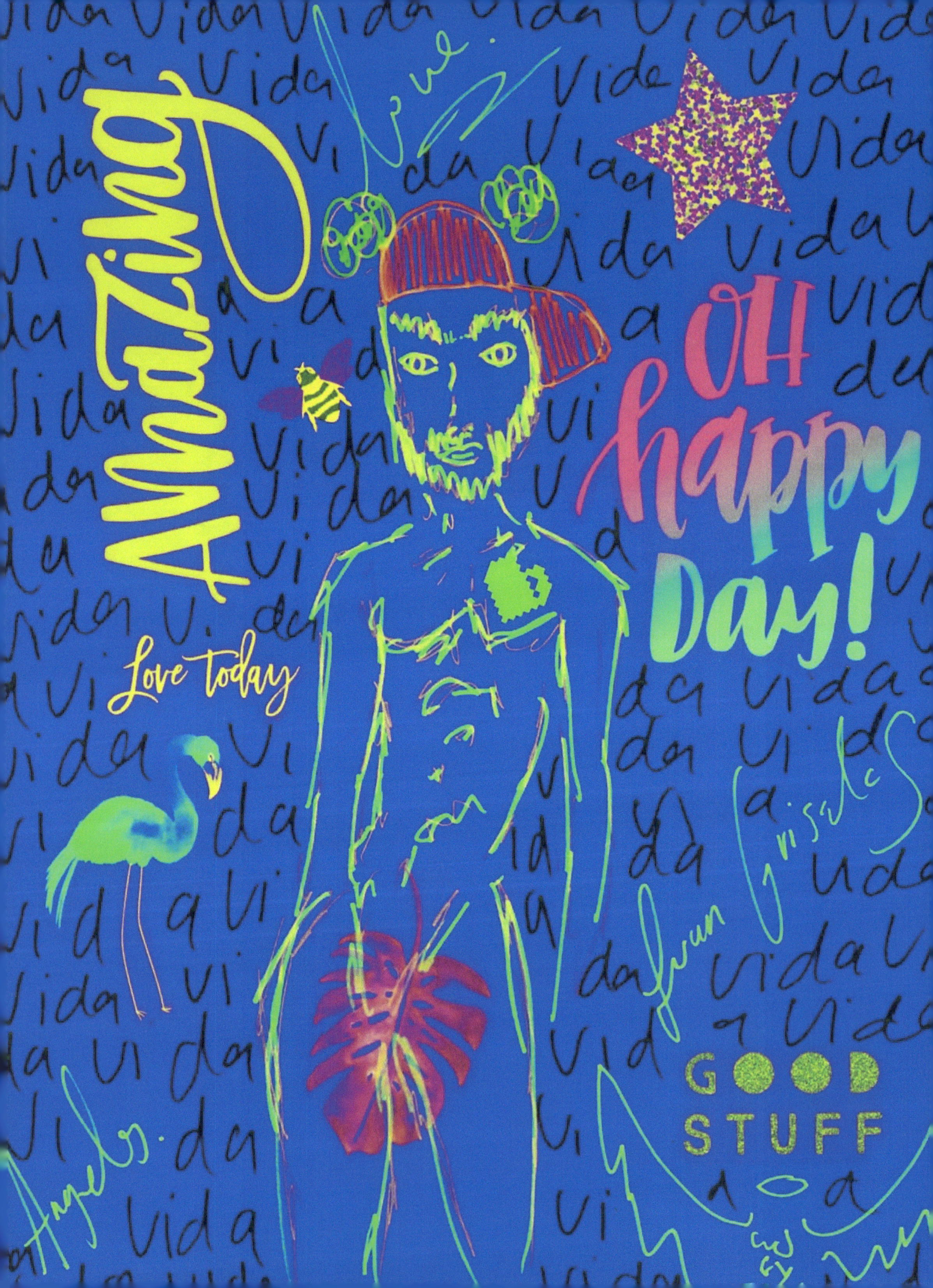

Amazing

OH happy Day!

Love today

GOOD STUFF

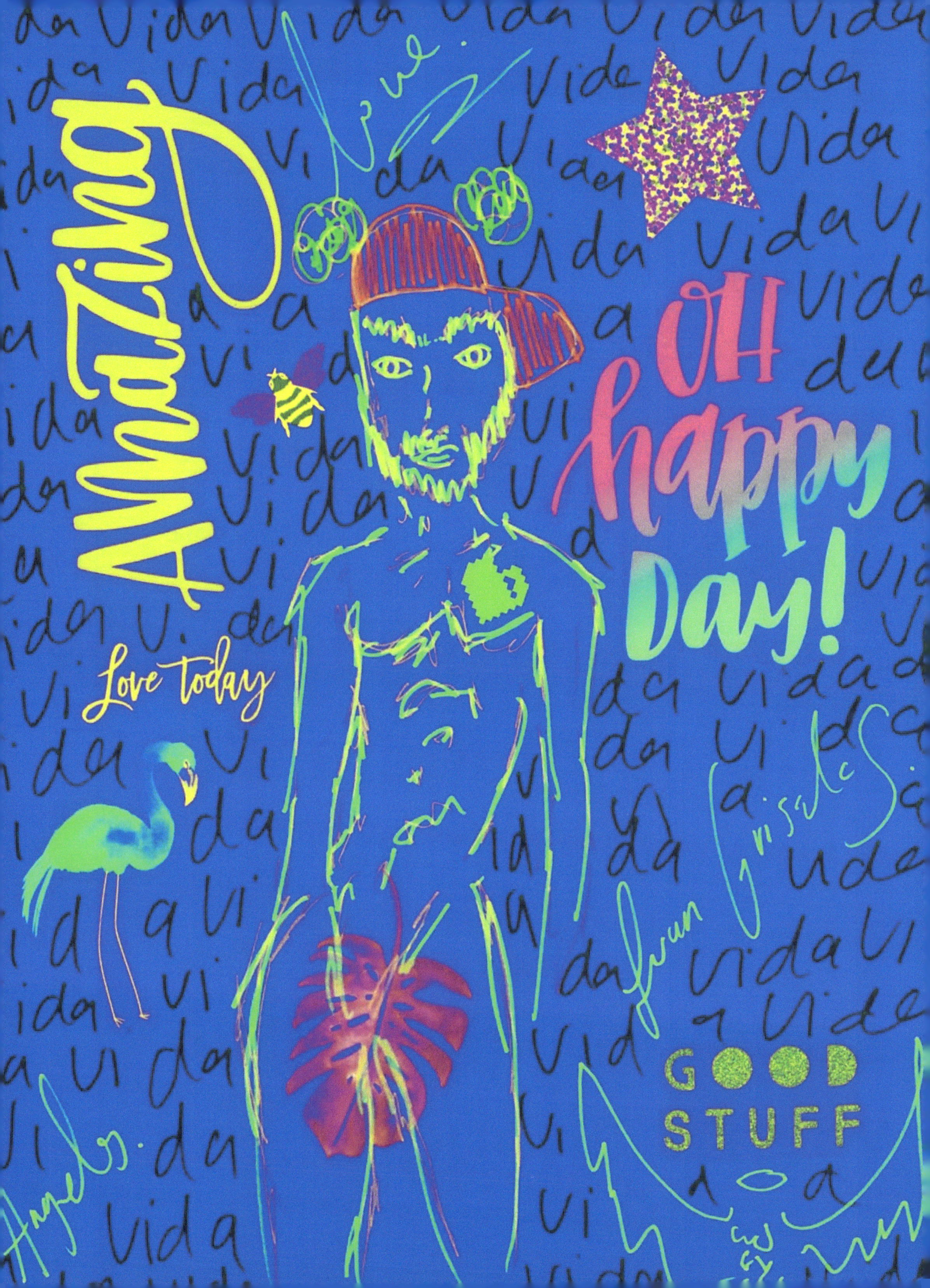

Amazing

OH happy Day!

Love today

GOOD STUFF

Juan knew nothing because he was born alone.
His mother was the Earth and his father was the Sun.
They were the greatest parents of them all.
They gave him everything, but somehow everything wasn't enough.

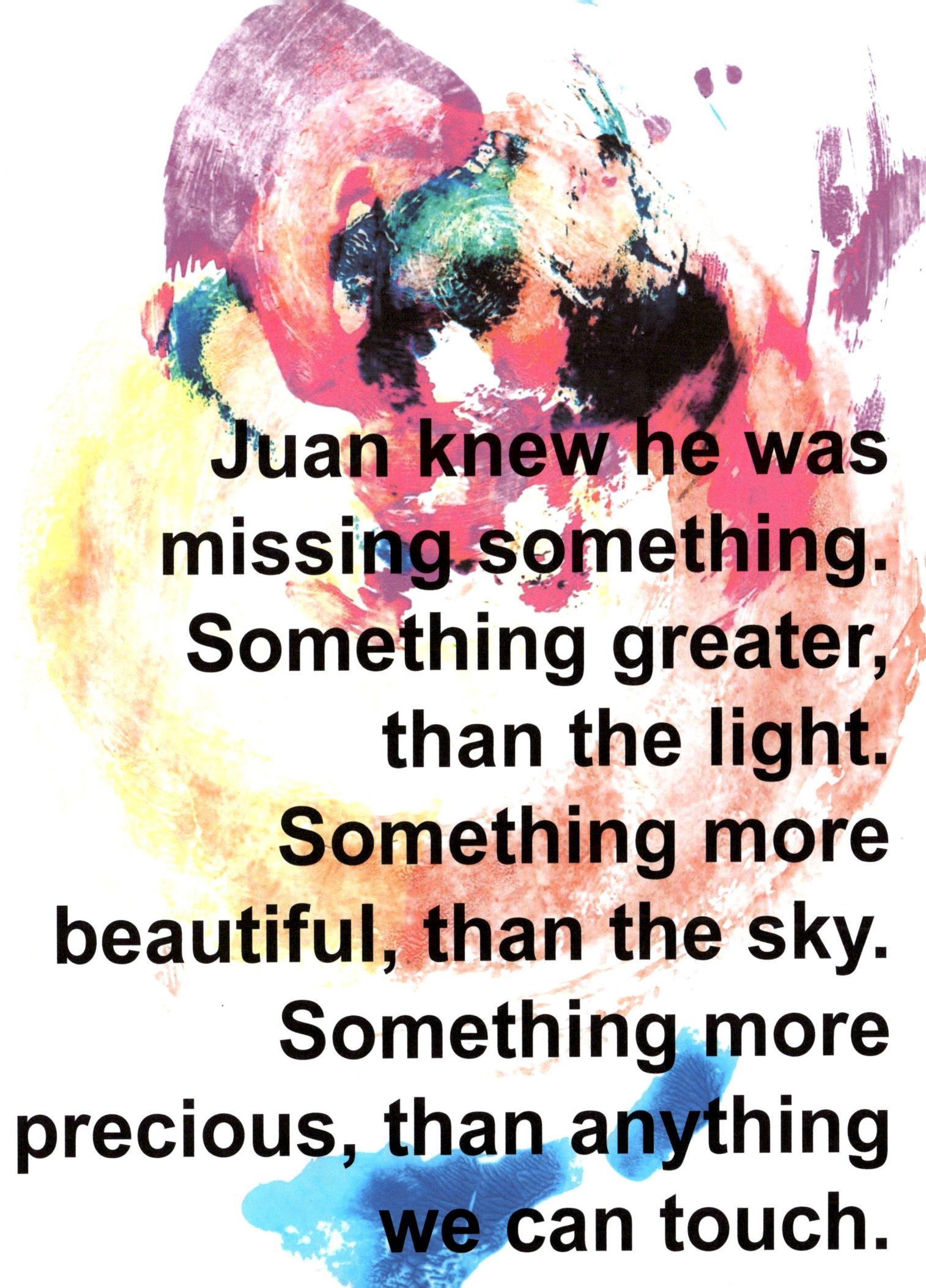

Juan knew he was missing something. Something greater, than the light. Something more beautiful, than the sky. Something more precious, than anything we can touch.

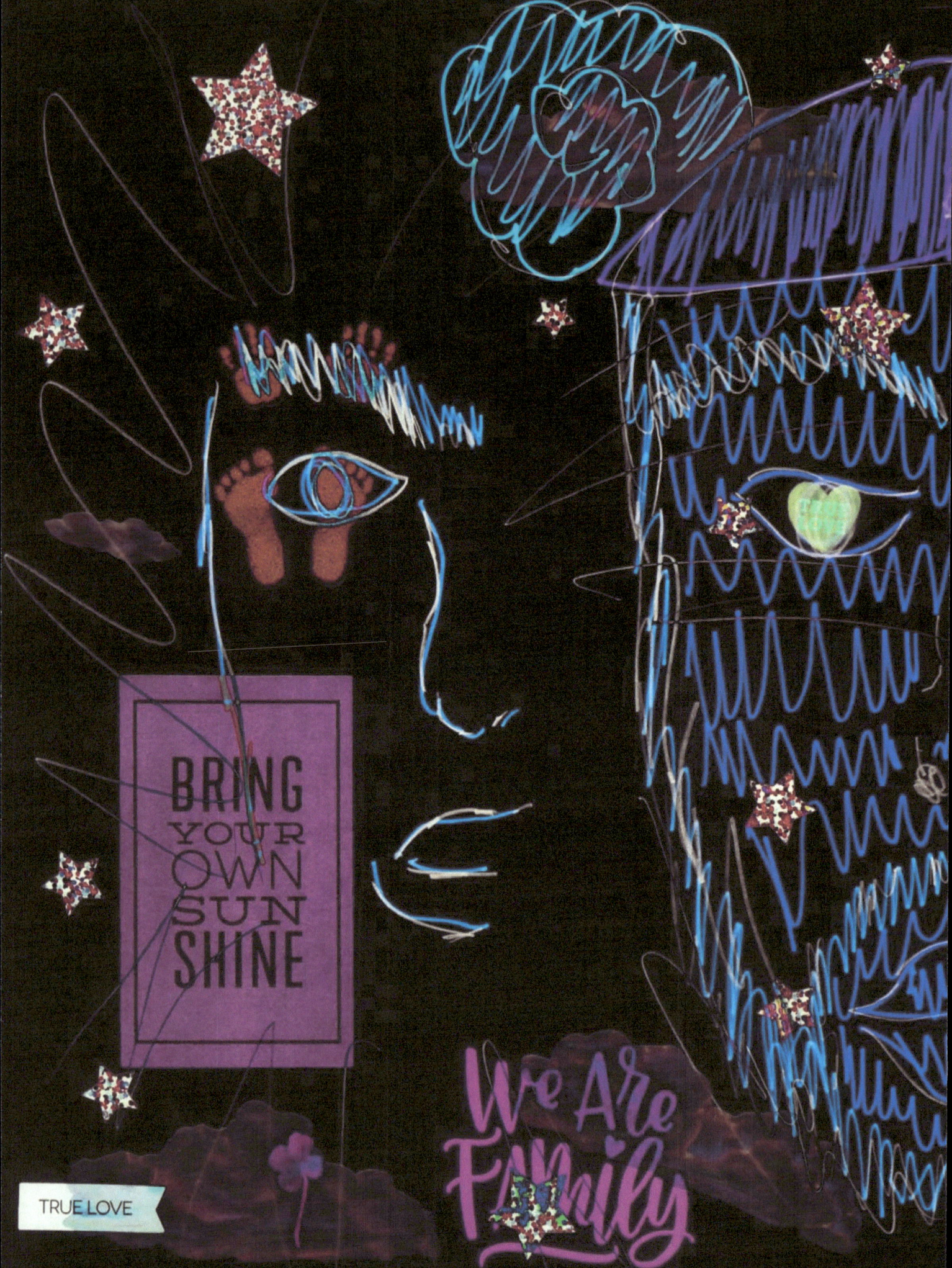

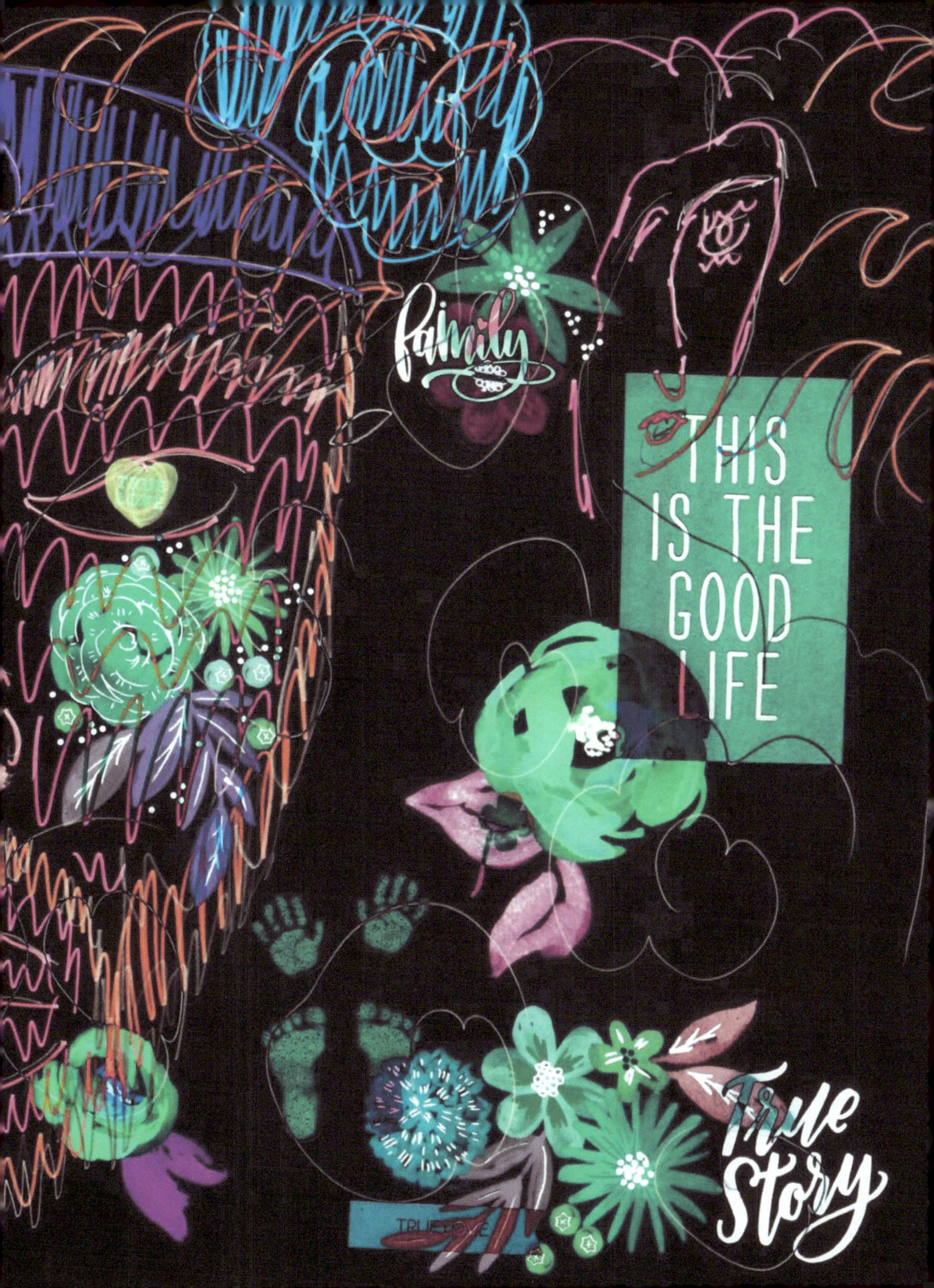

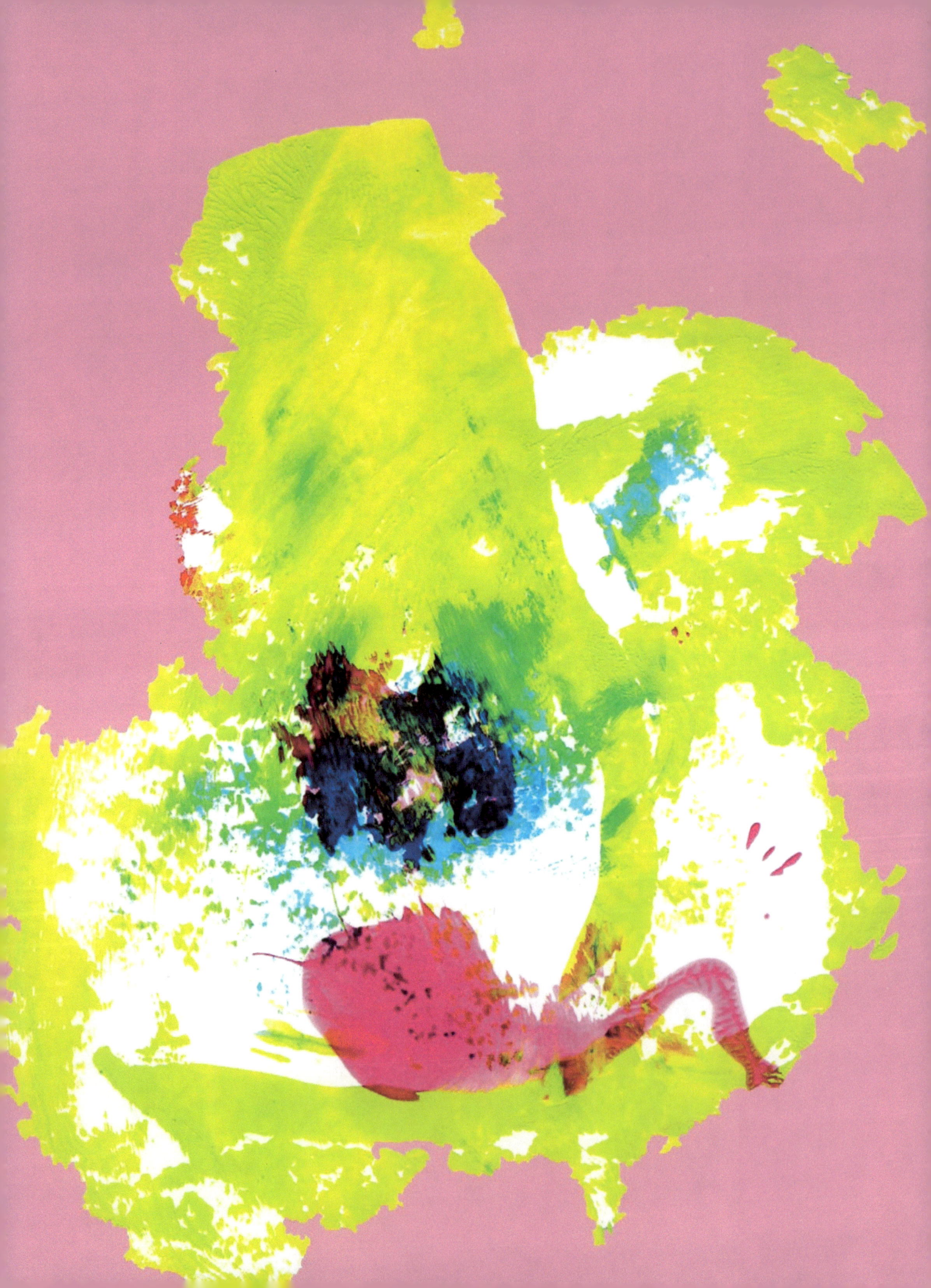

So Juan ran away.
He ran fast and far.
He ran to a place where his father and mother couldn't find him.

He ran away from the place where he was given everything.

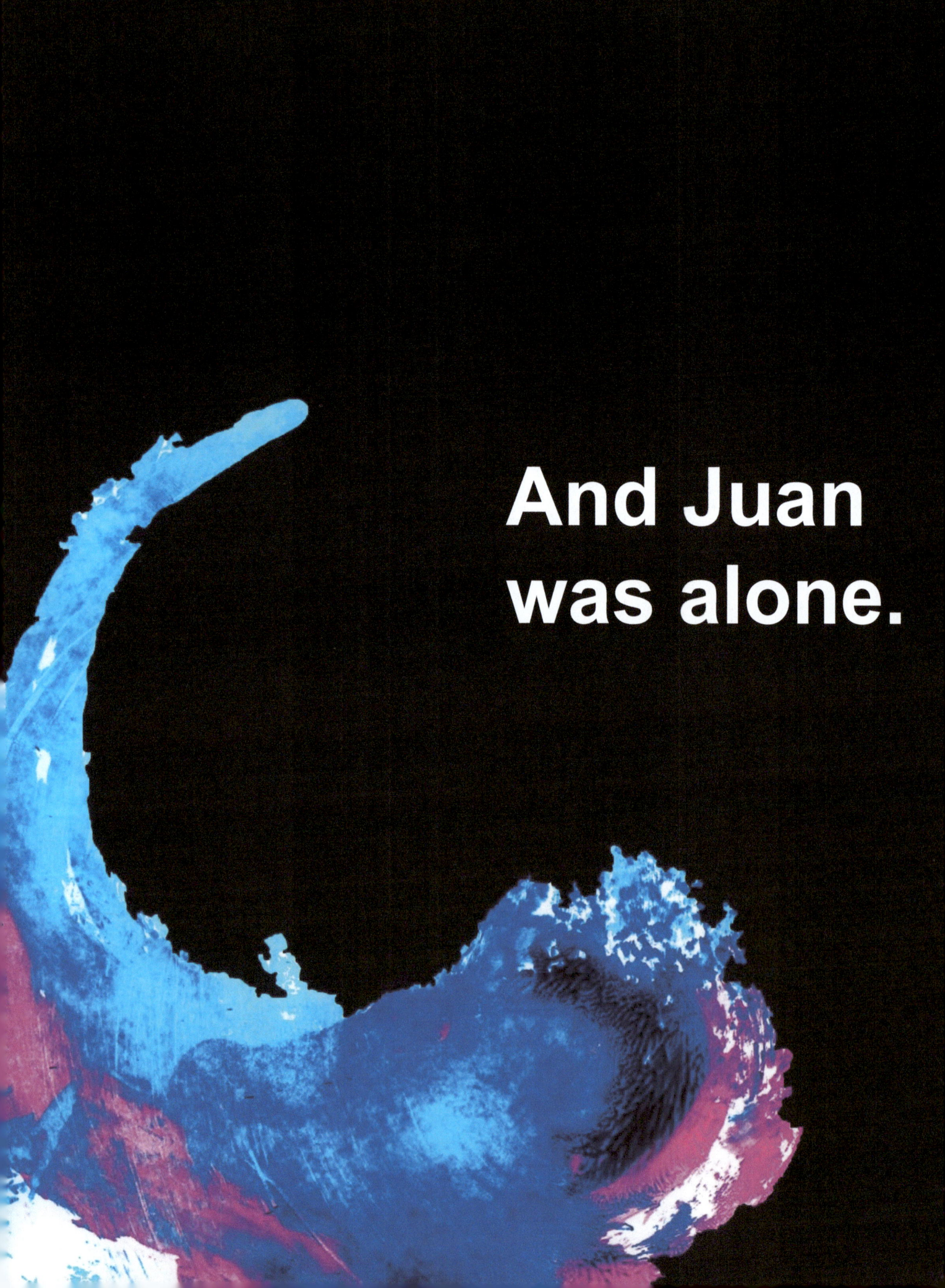

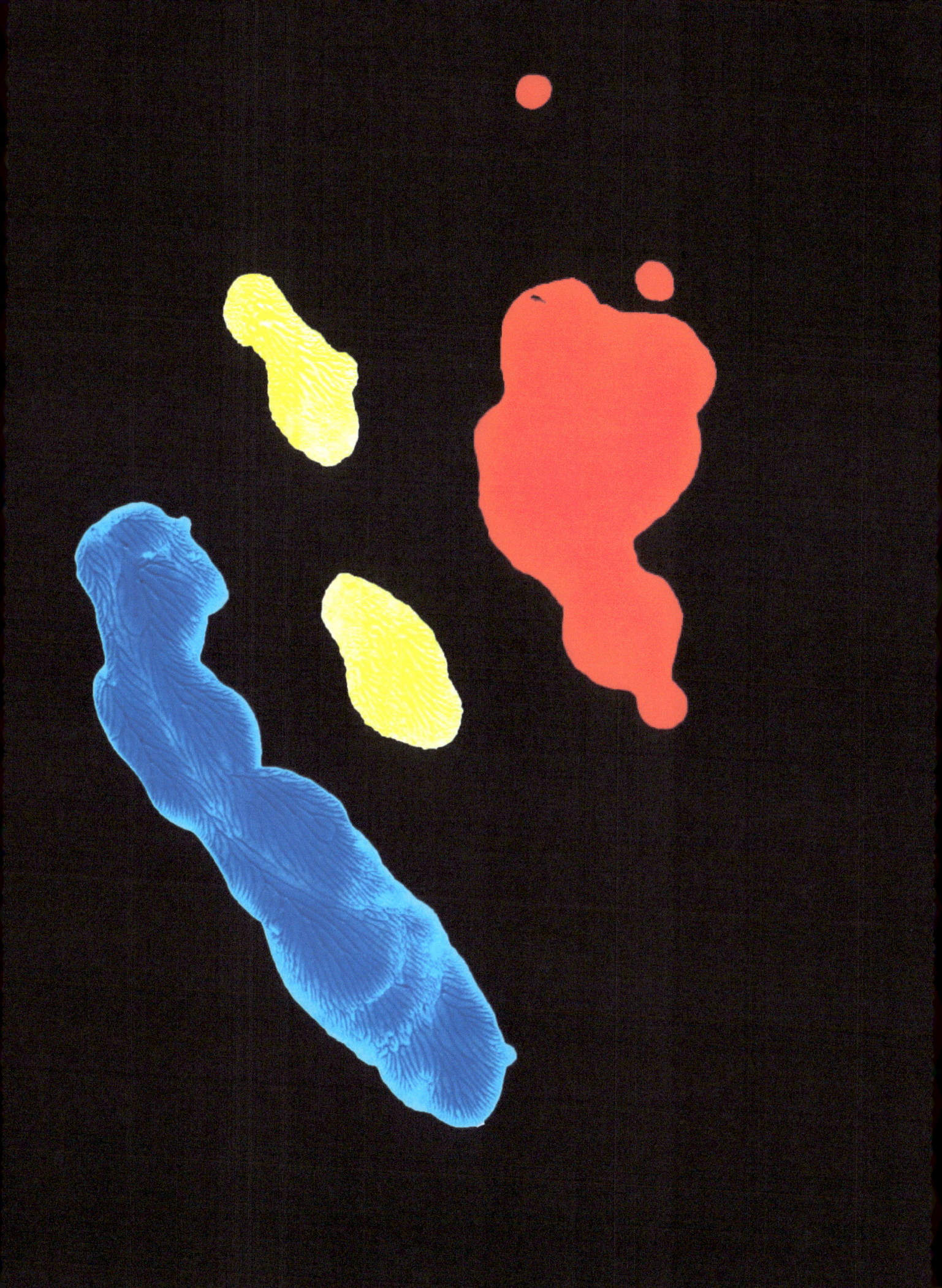

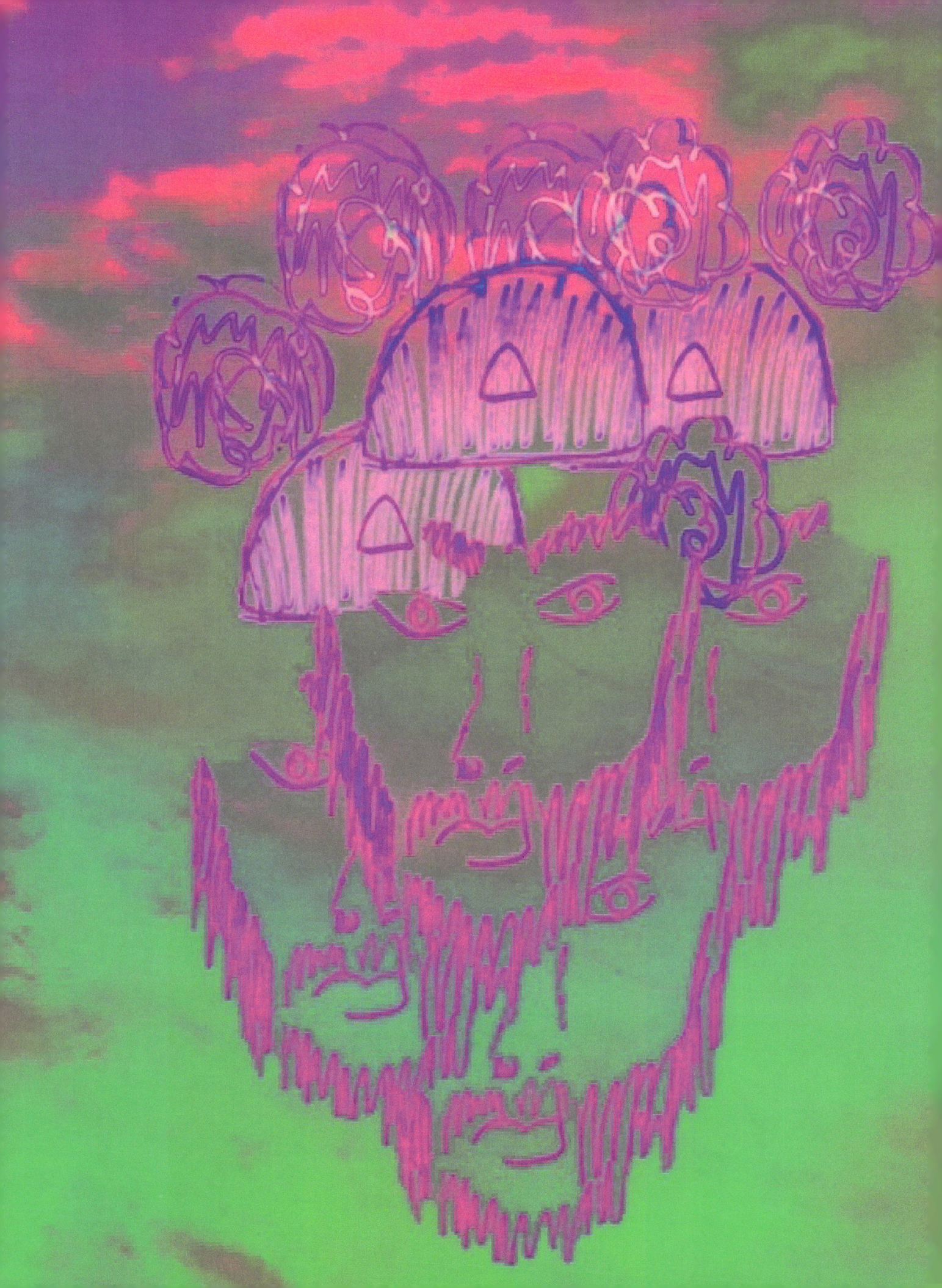

In the dark, Juan wandered and wandered. He wandered a lot. He didn't know what he was doing.

It was his first time on his own.

Where am I?
What is this
strange place?
Juan asked himself.
This place was
like no other.
It's a place you can
only imagine
when you close
your eyes,
and you are left alone.

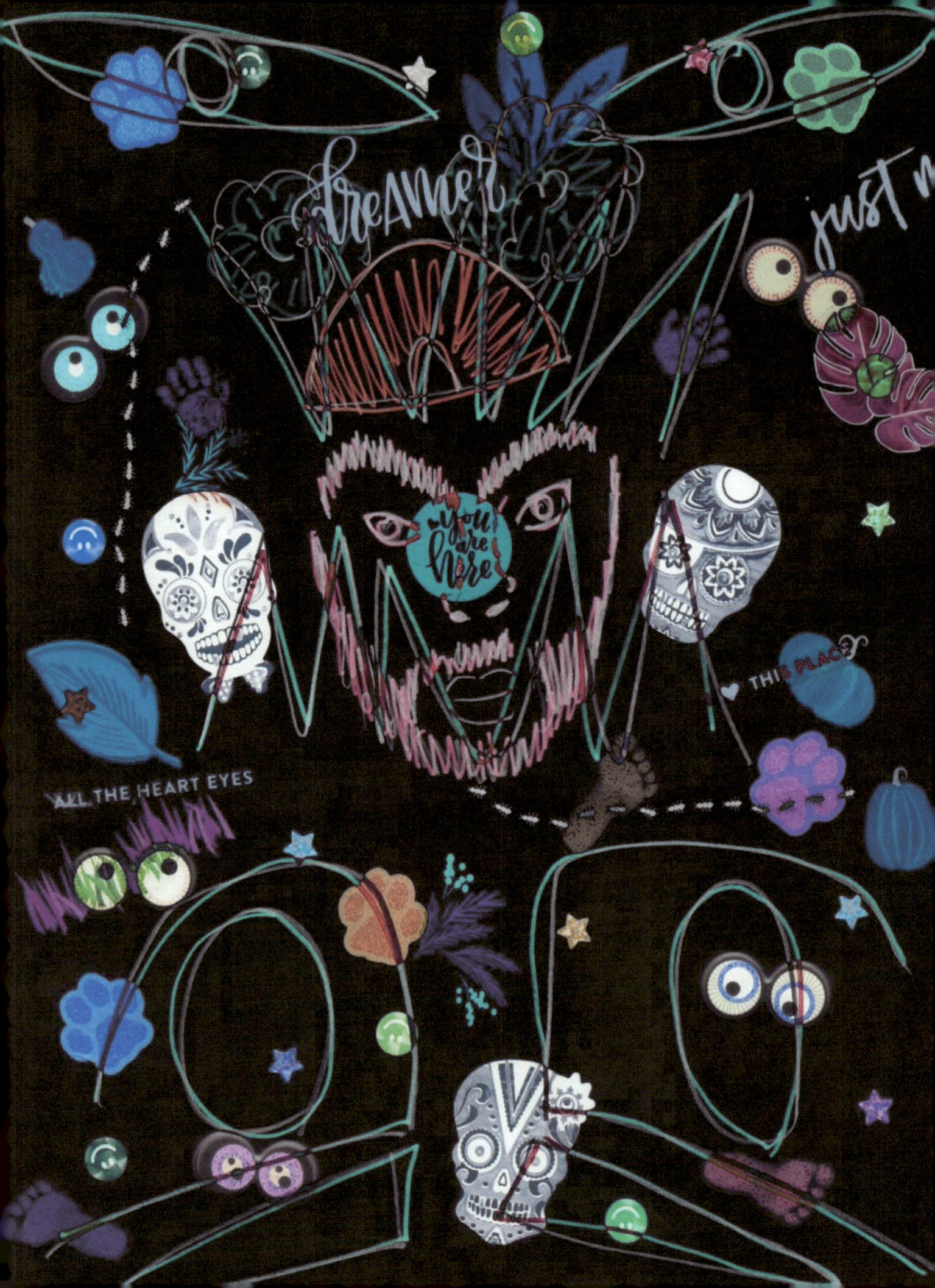

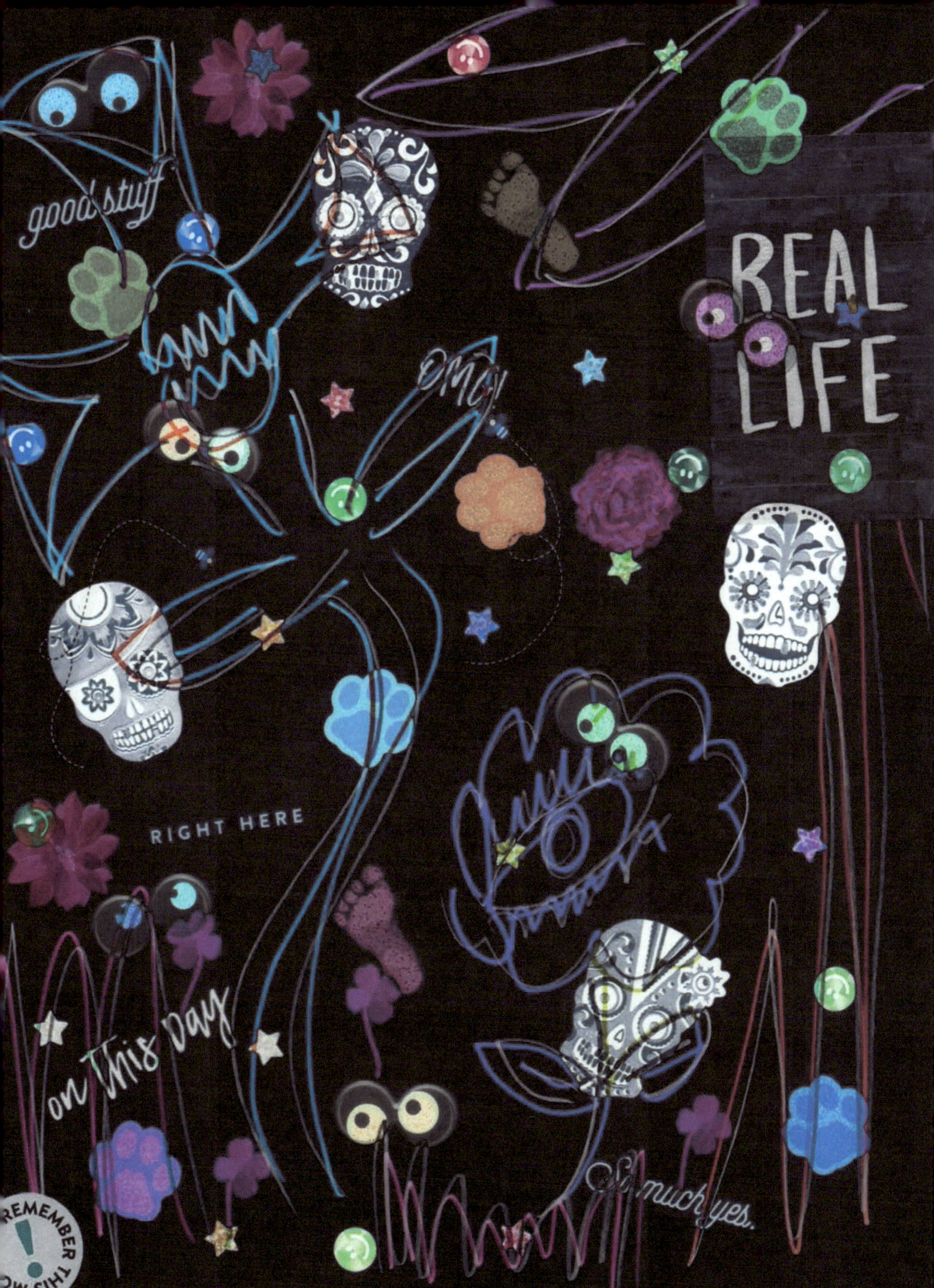

Because Juan was alone.

Or so he thought.

In the dark, he saw something.

Something you can only see in the dark.

So Juan approached it.

Because Juan was alone.

Who are you?
Juan asked.

My name is Anger.
Anger said.
Anger was big.
Very big, Very very big,
Very very very big.
Anger was somebody who looked like he could take care of himself.
Anger didn't need no parents.
Anger was too big for that.

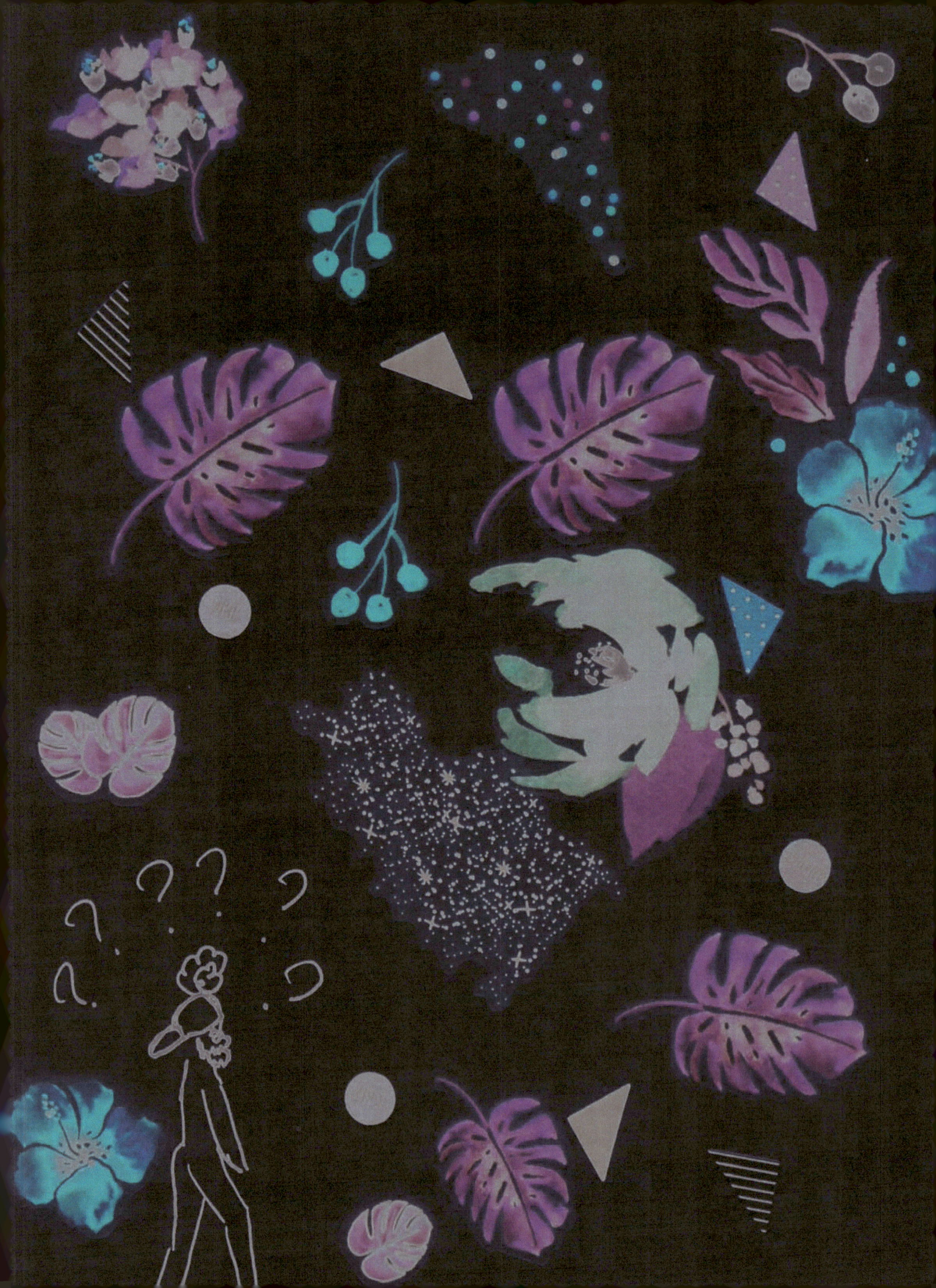

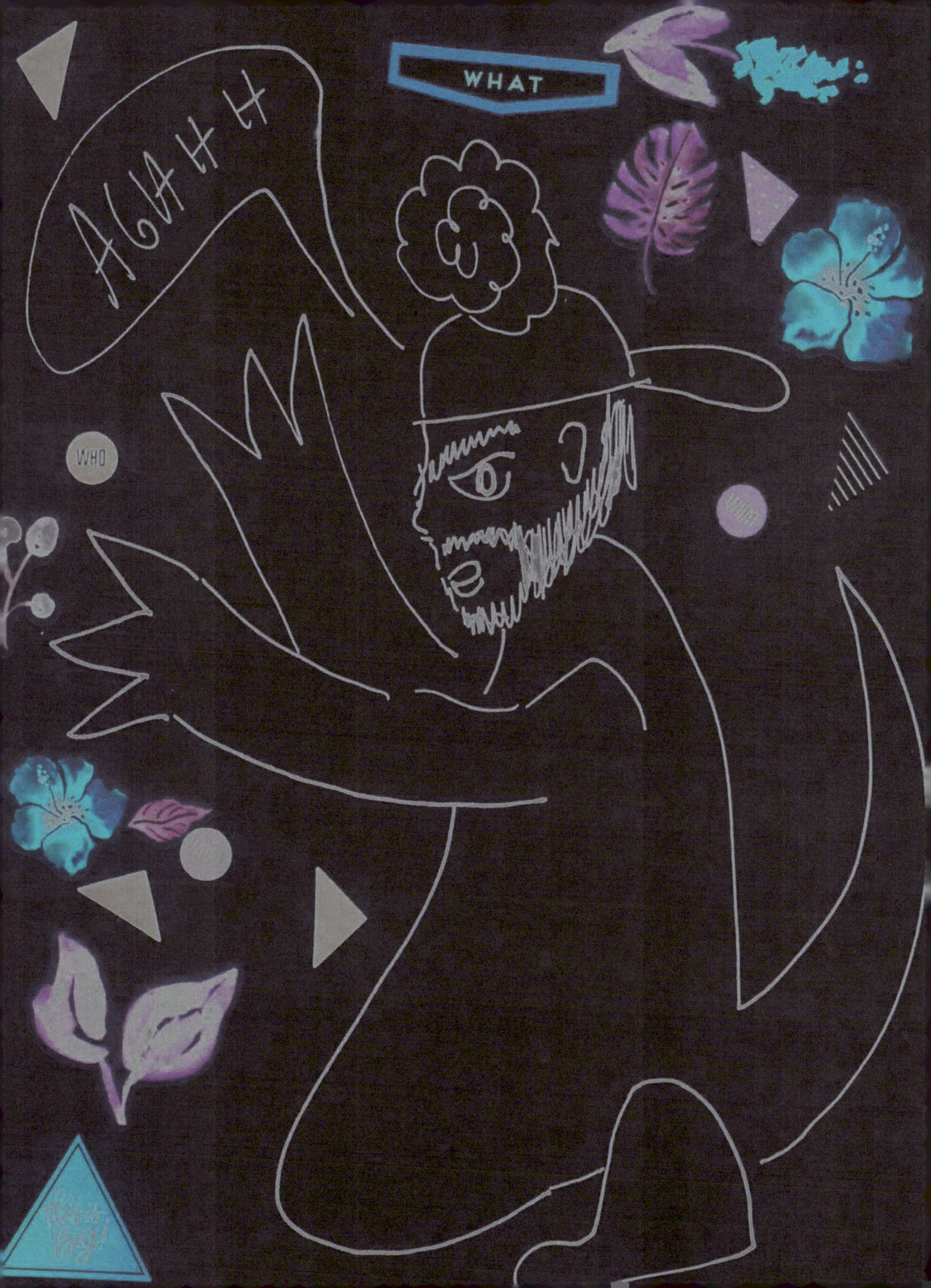

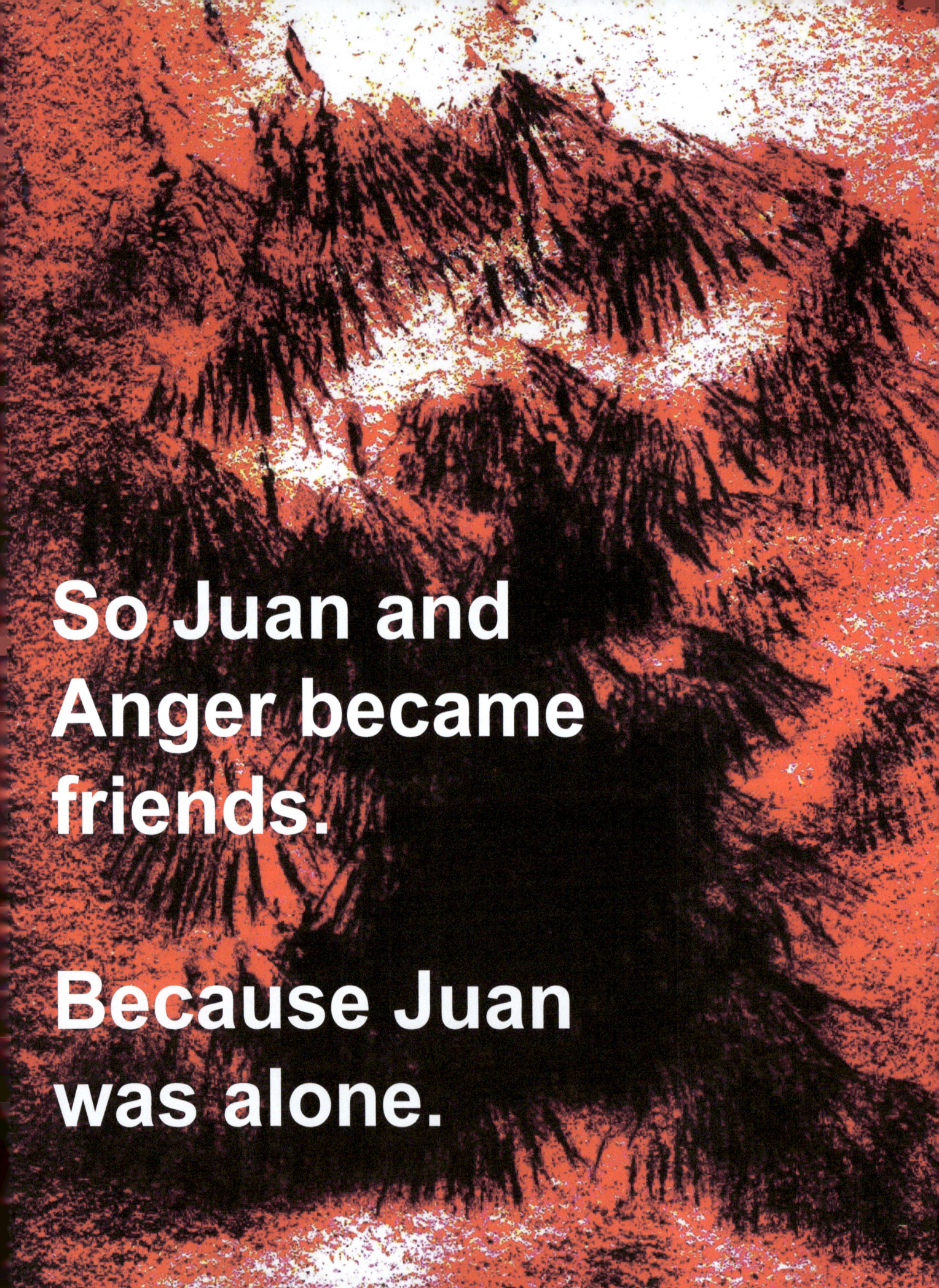

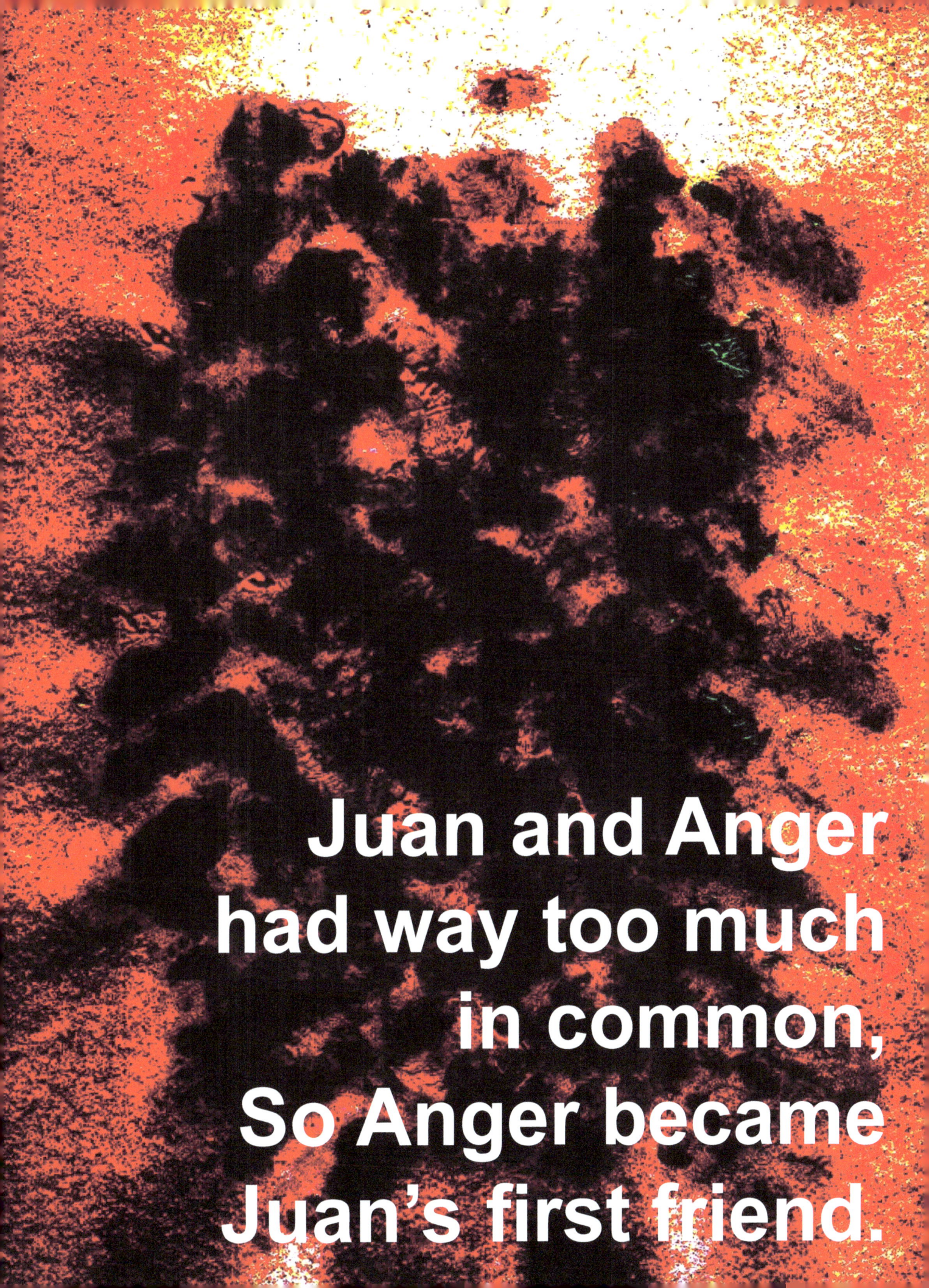

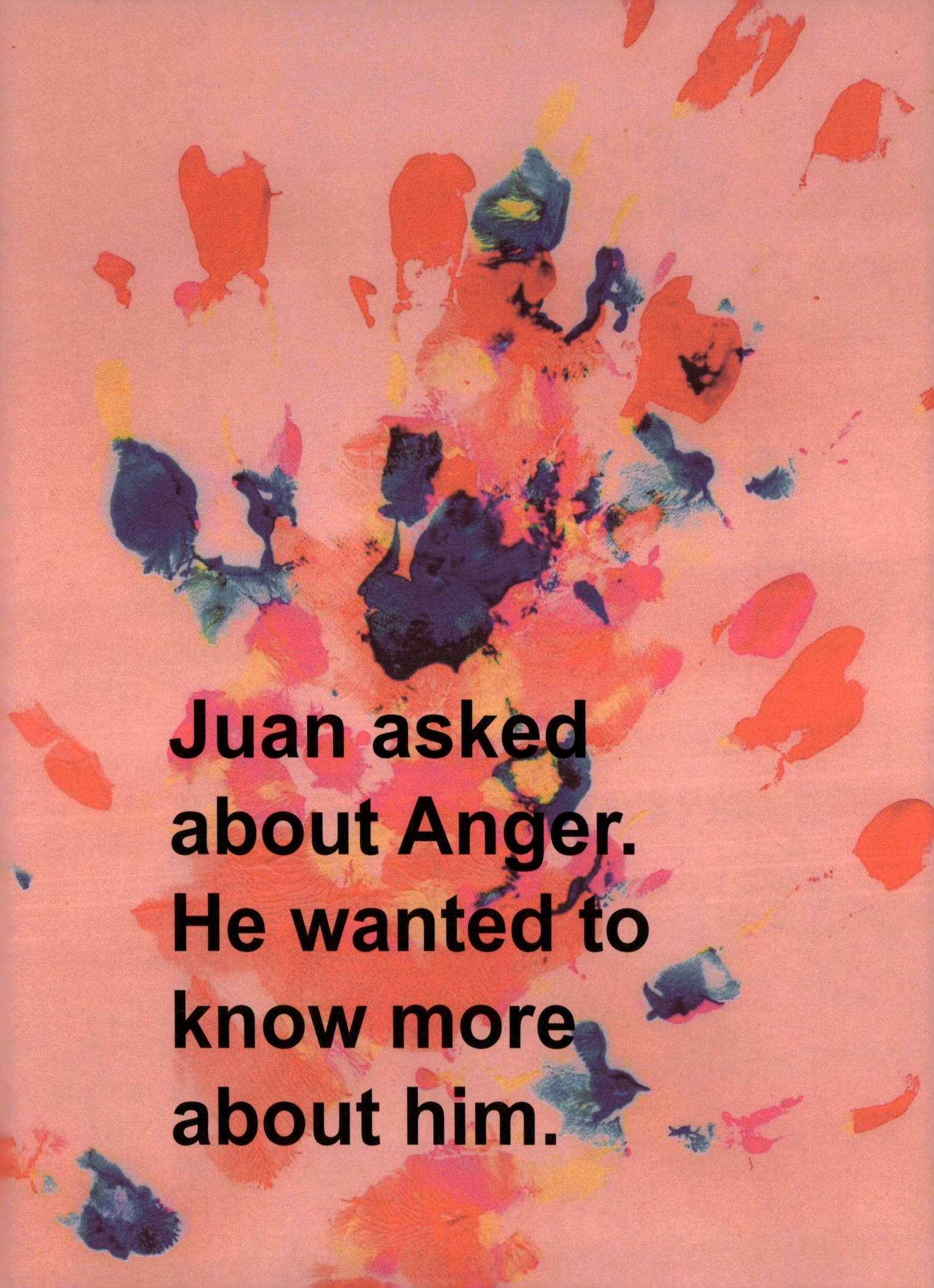

I am Anger. Anger said. I am very very very big, and I only get bigger and bigger. In the dark, I like to wander. Like all fun stuff do. Because everything cool happens in the dark. I only show up when something good is about to happen.

When I show up, I observe. And I say no words. I don't let anyone notice me, but at some point, someone notices me. Sooner, than later, they notice me because I'm very very very big.

And when they notice me, It's already too late for me to walk away.

Because I'm very very very big, they always start yelling at me. They throw stuff at me, And they don't treat me nice.

But you see, when they don't treat me nice, I only get bigger and bigger.

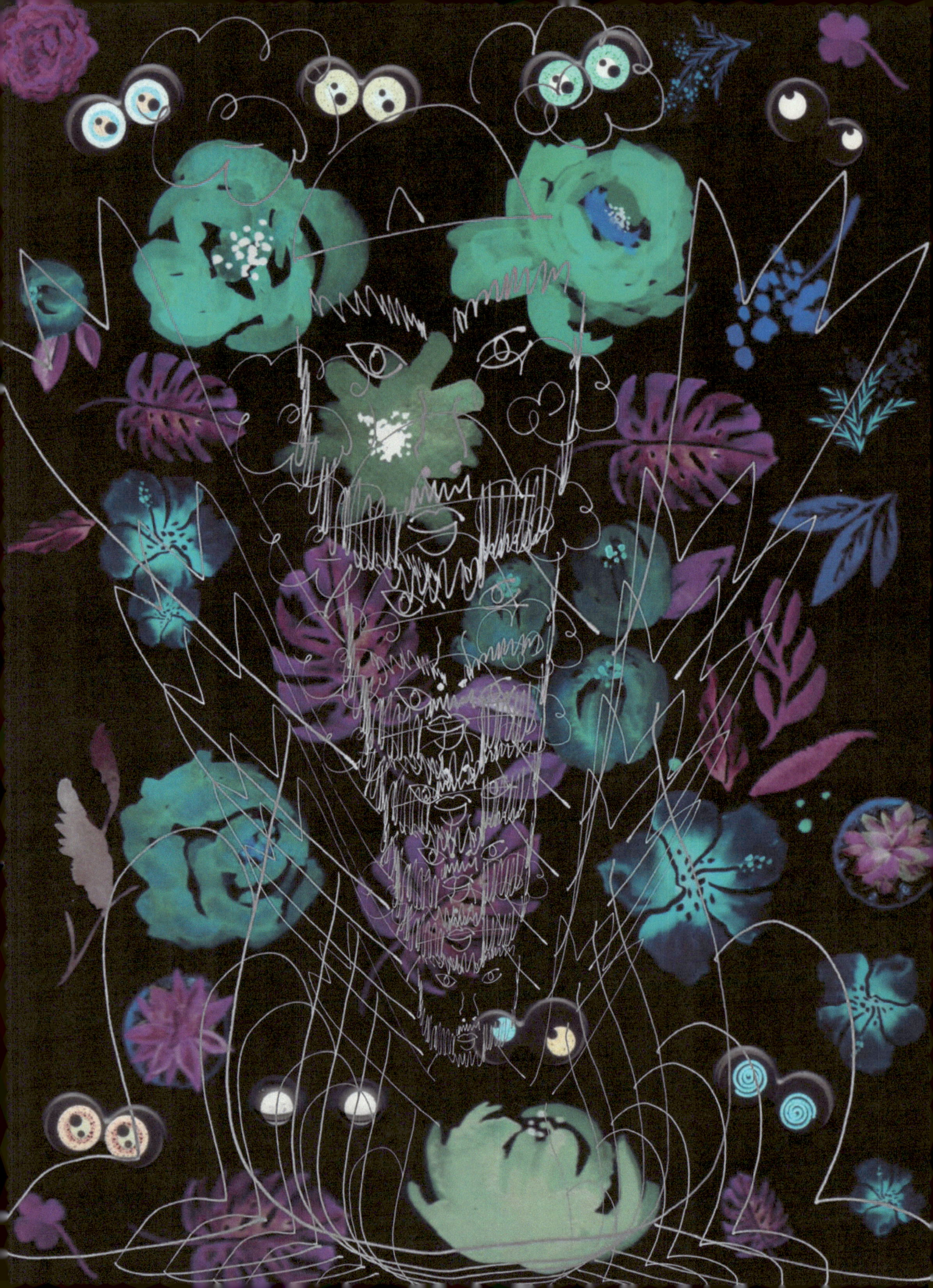

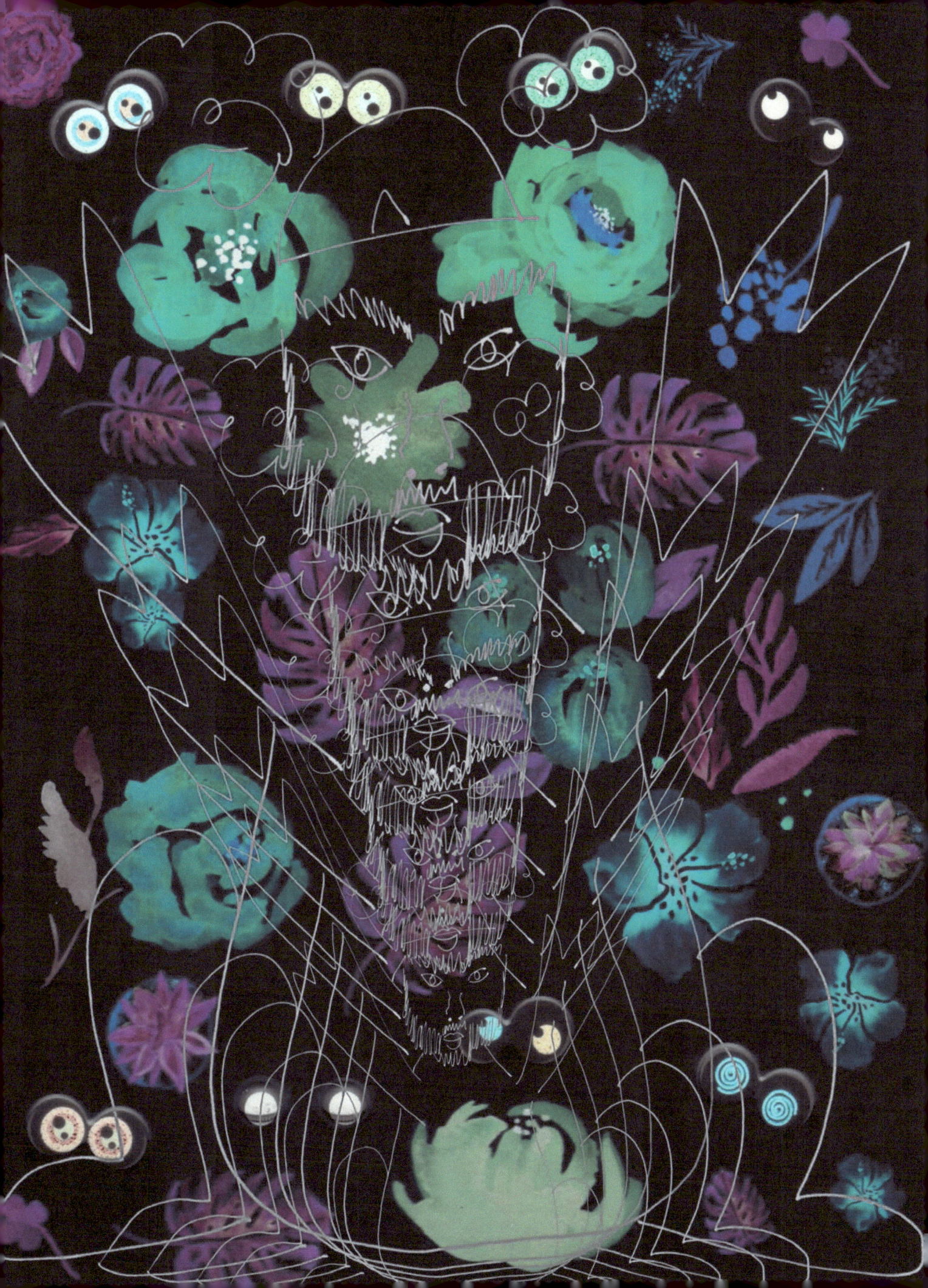

Then, they realize
they cannot fight me,
So they make me pick
their side.
You see, how I only
get bigger and bigger,
They always want me
in their team.

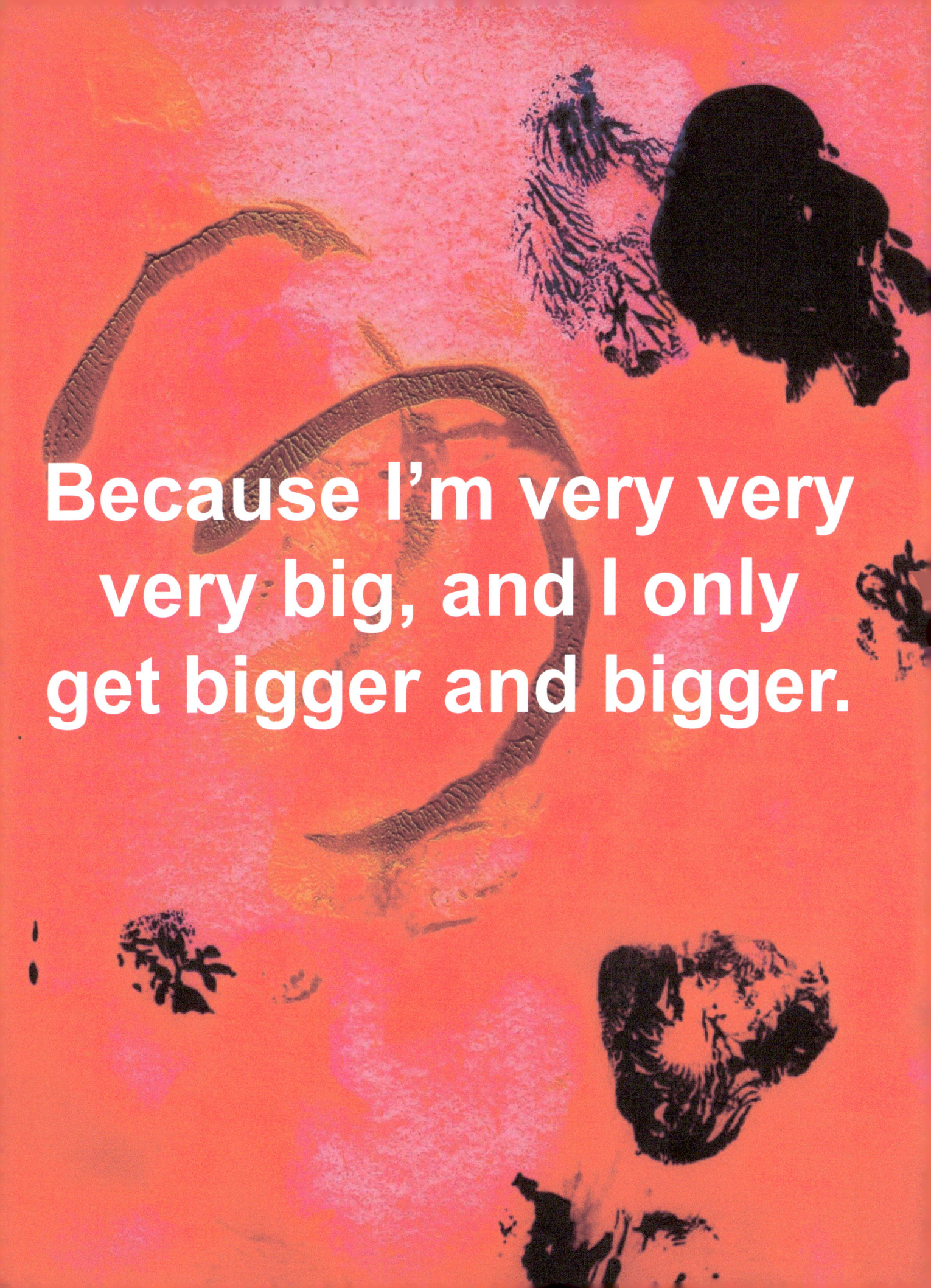

So when I play
in your team,
For sure,
that team will win.
And you see,
you don't have to
worry about me.
I can take care
of myself

Because I'm very very
very big, and I only get
bigger and bigger.

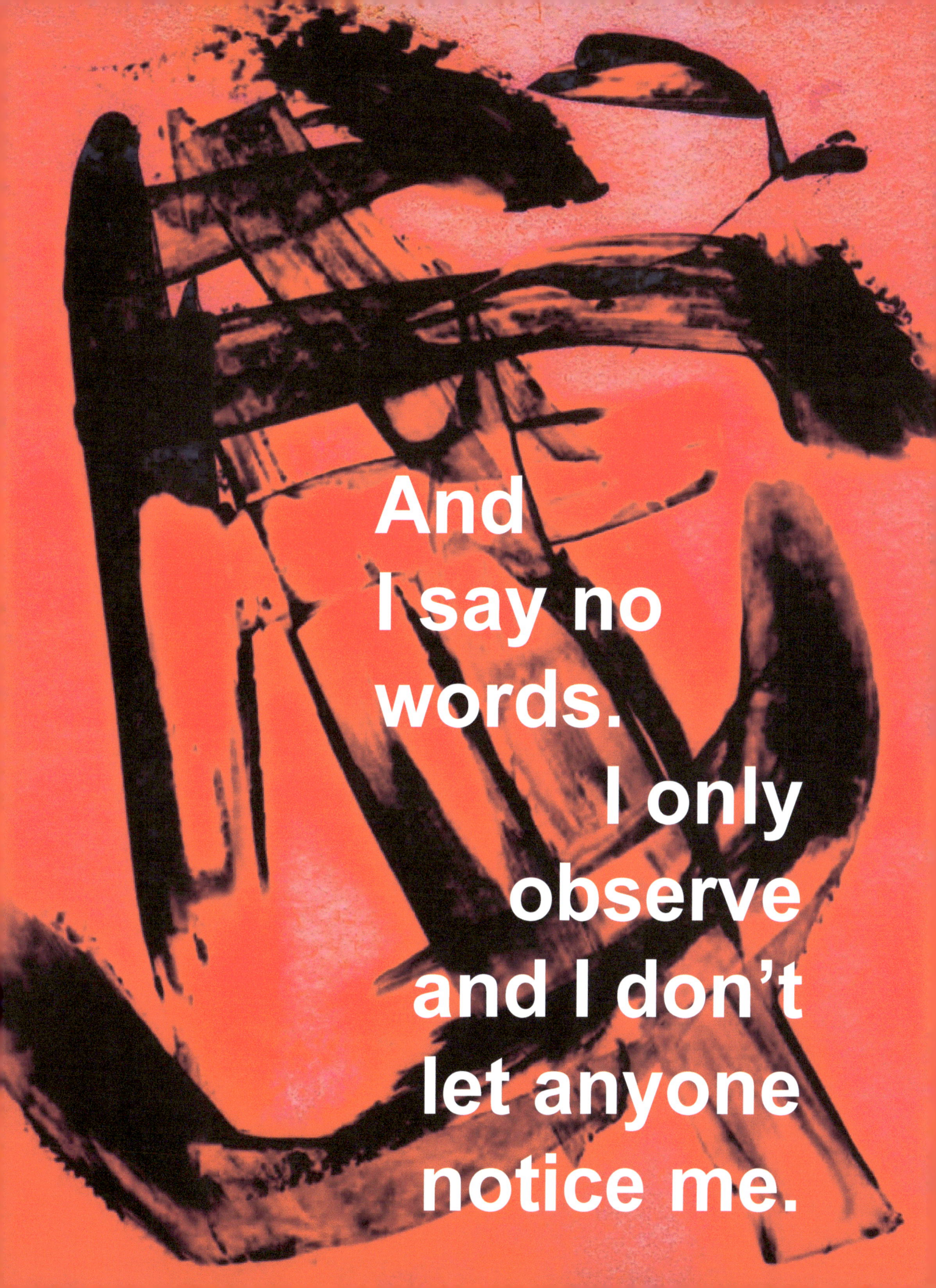

Suddenly, as Anger said these last words. That, what you can only see in the dark, You couldn't see no more!

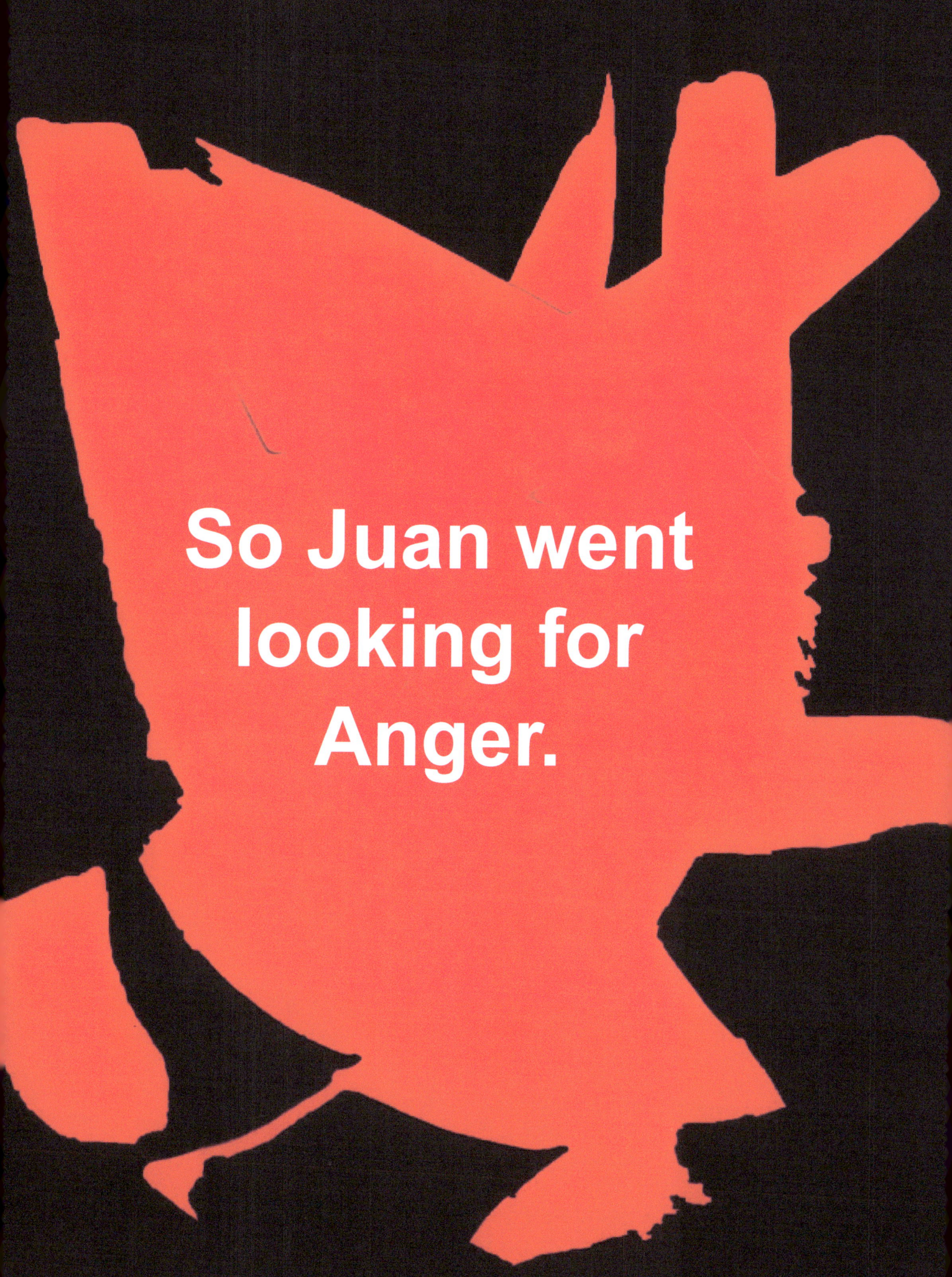

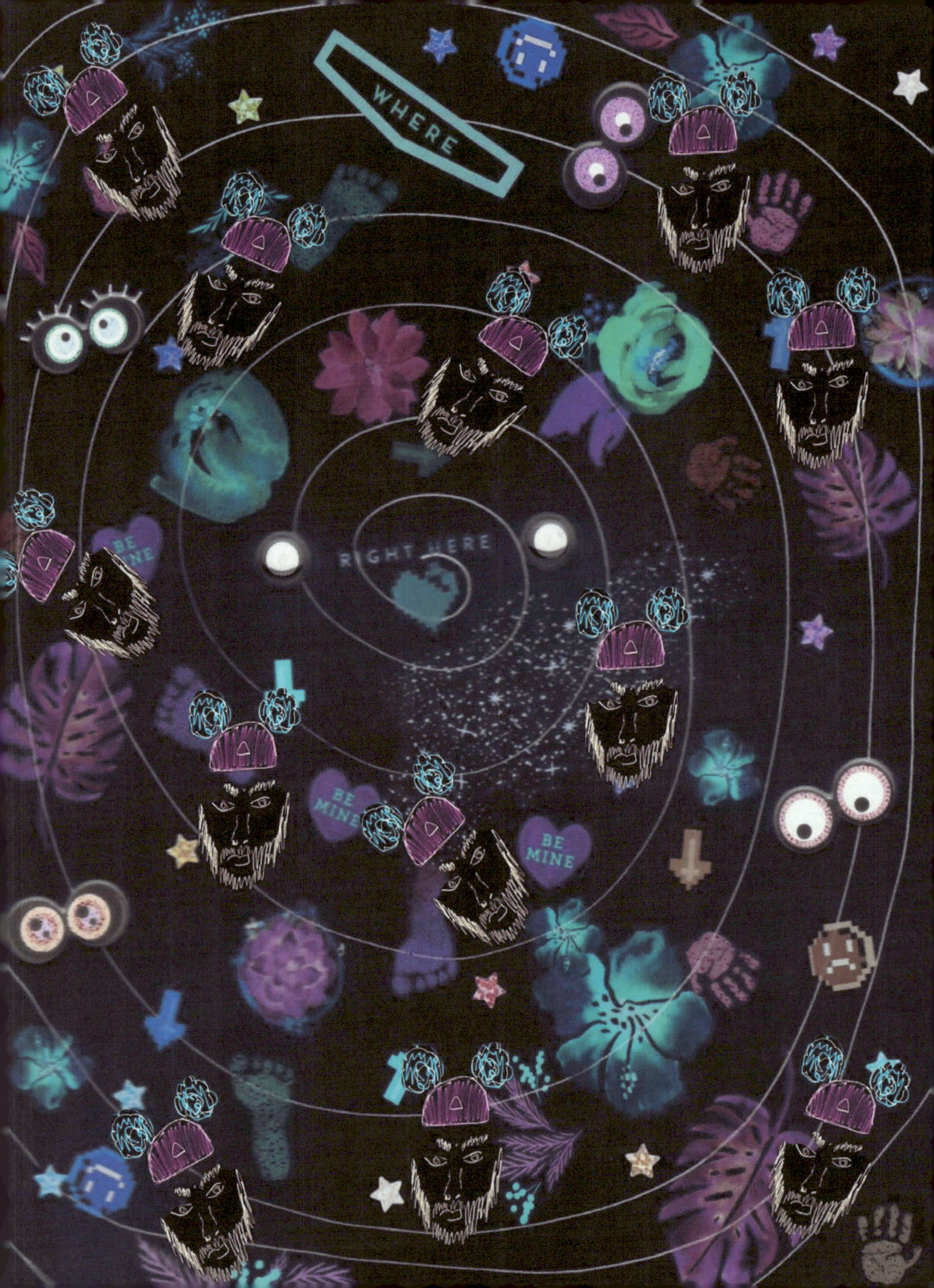

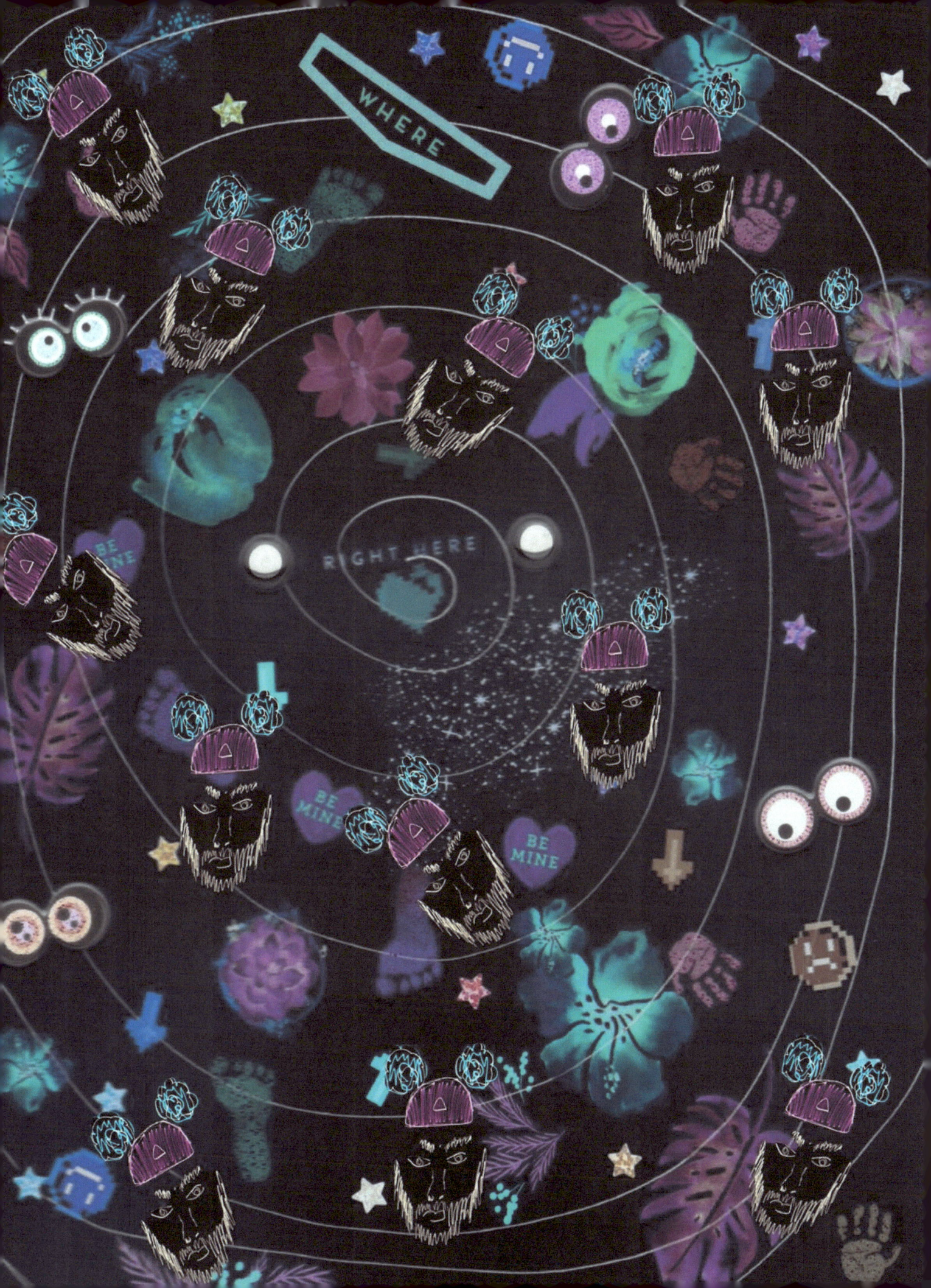

In the dark, Juan wandered and wandered. He wandered a lot. But Juan could not seem to notice Anger.

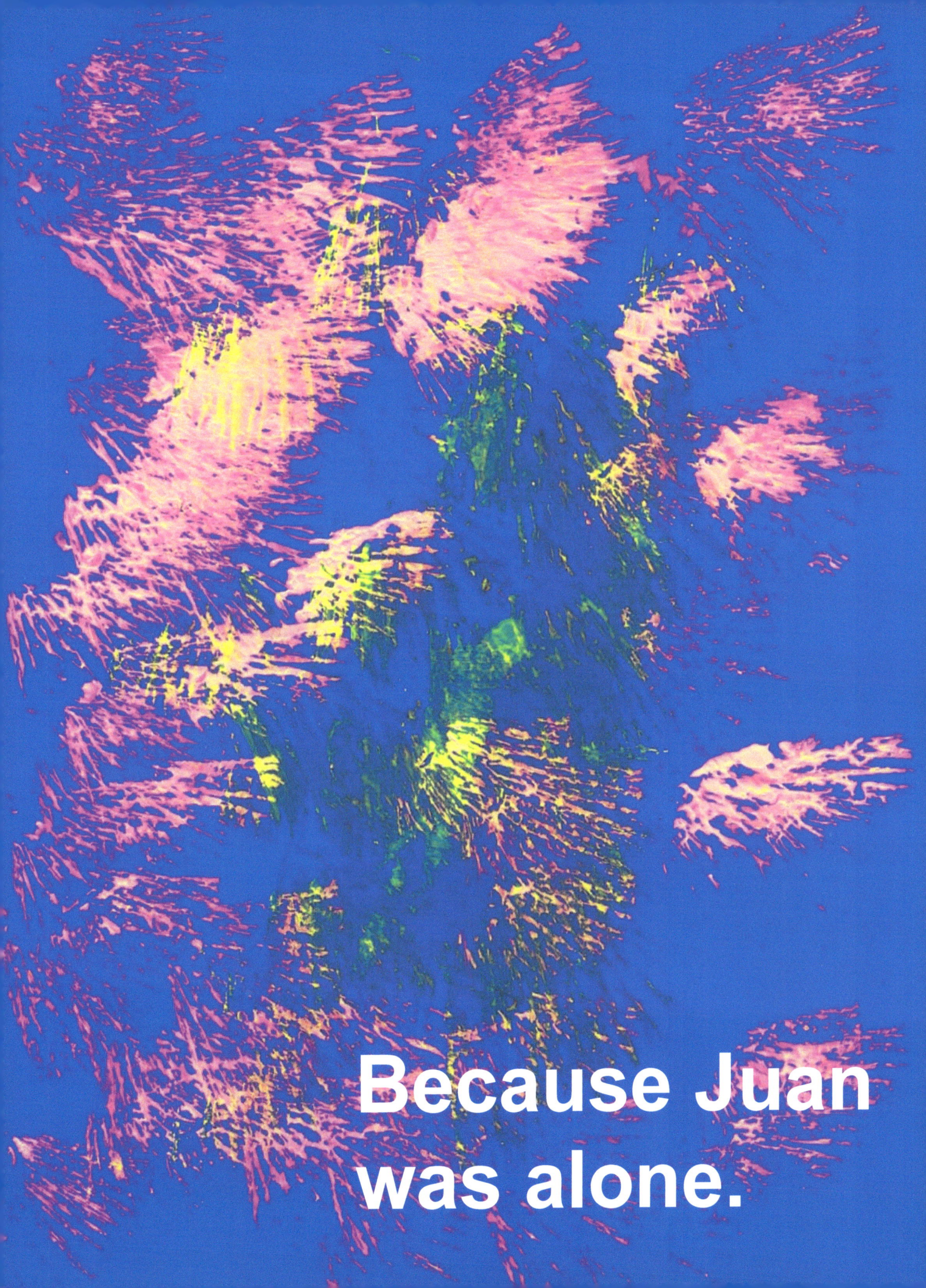

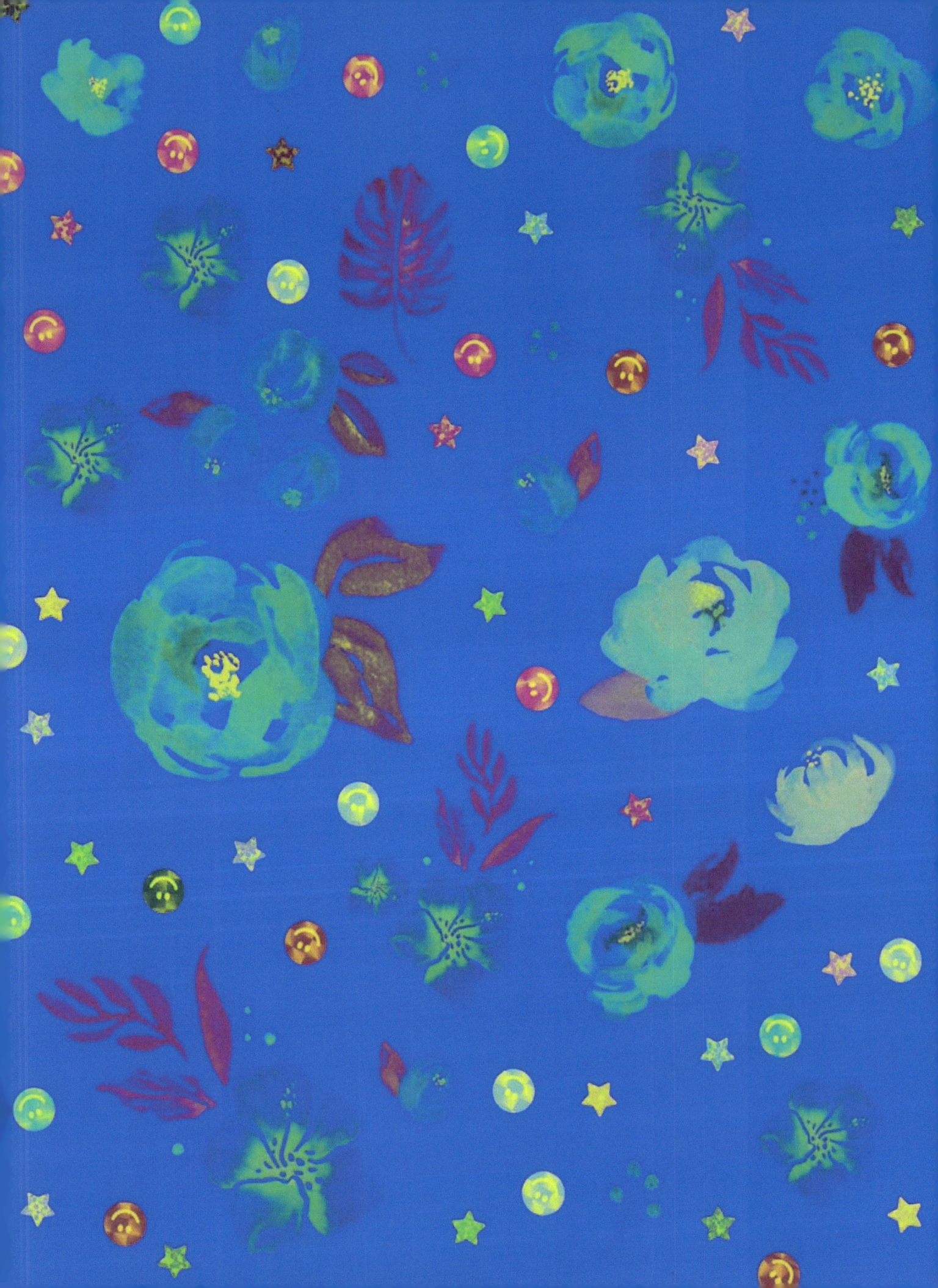

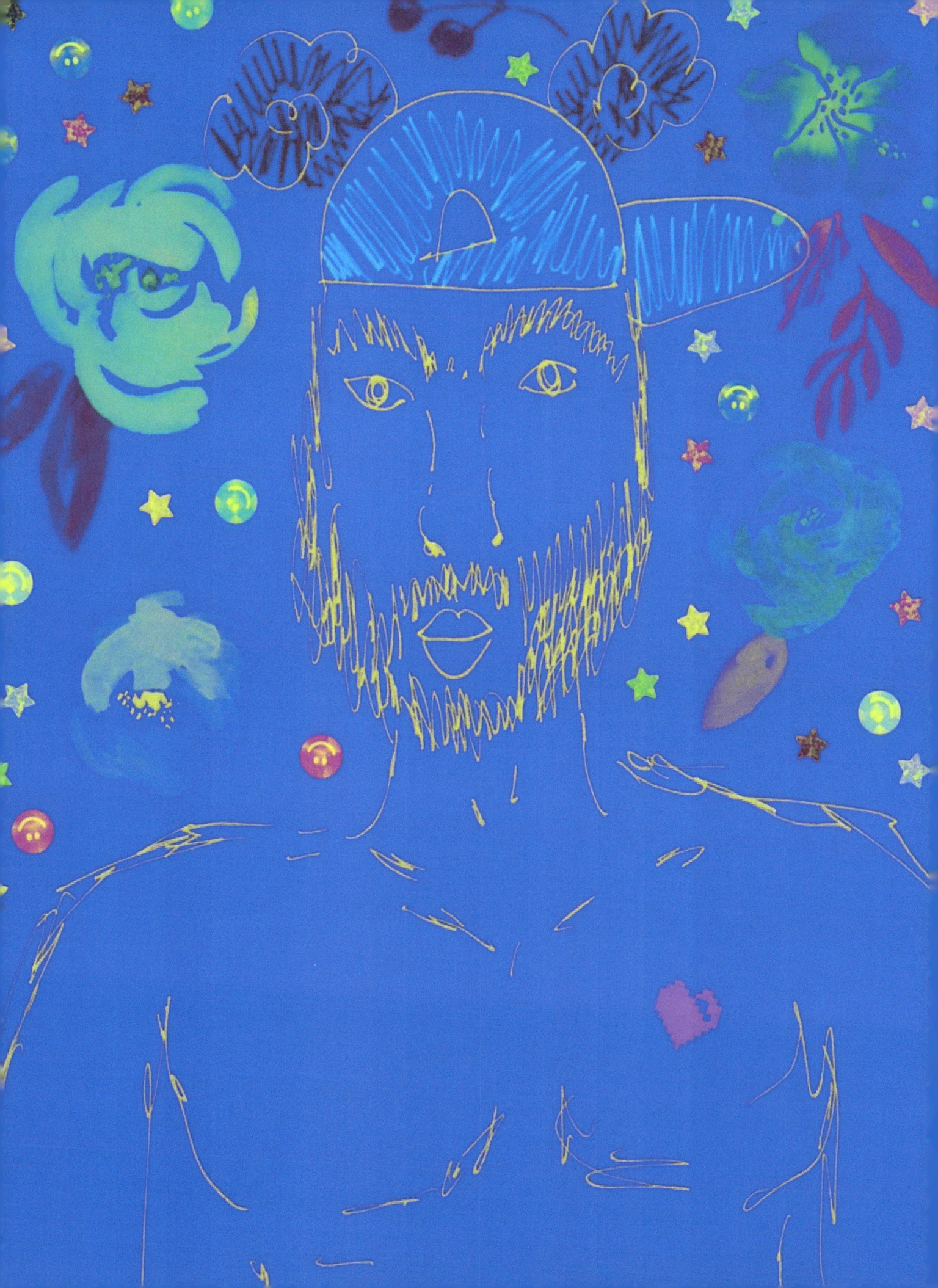

In the dark, Juan saw a little something in the distance.

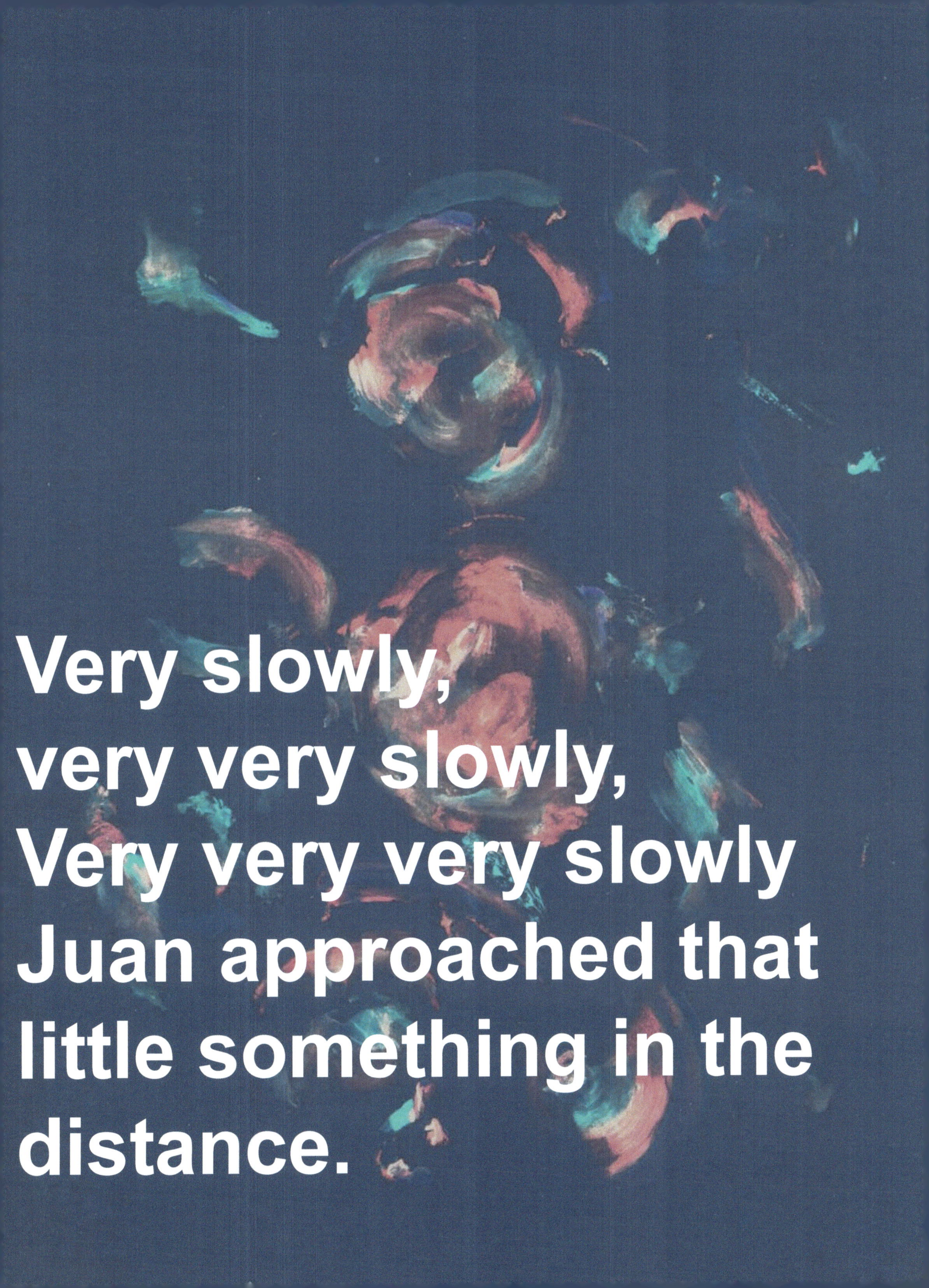

Very slowly,
very very slowly,
Very very very slowly
Juan approached that
little something in the
distance.

That little something in the distance was very very very small. Juan didn't know what that little something in the distance was. So Juan poked that little something in the distance with his pinky finger. And that little something in the distance got tickled.

Hi, my name is Fear.
That little something in the distance, said.
Fear? What? What are you? Juan asked.
I'm like a feeling, Fear said.
You know, like the feelings that you feel. Get it?

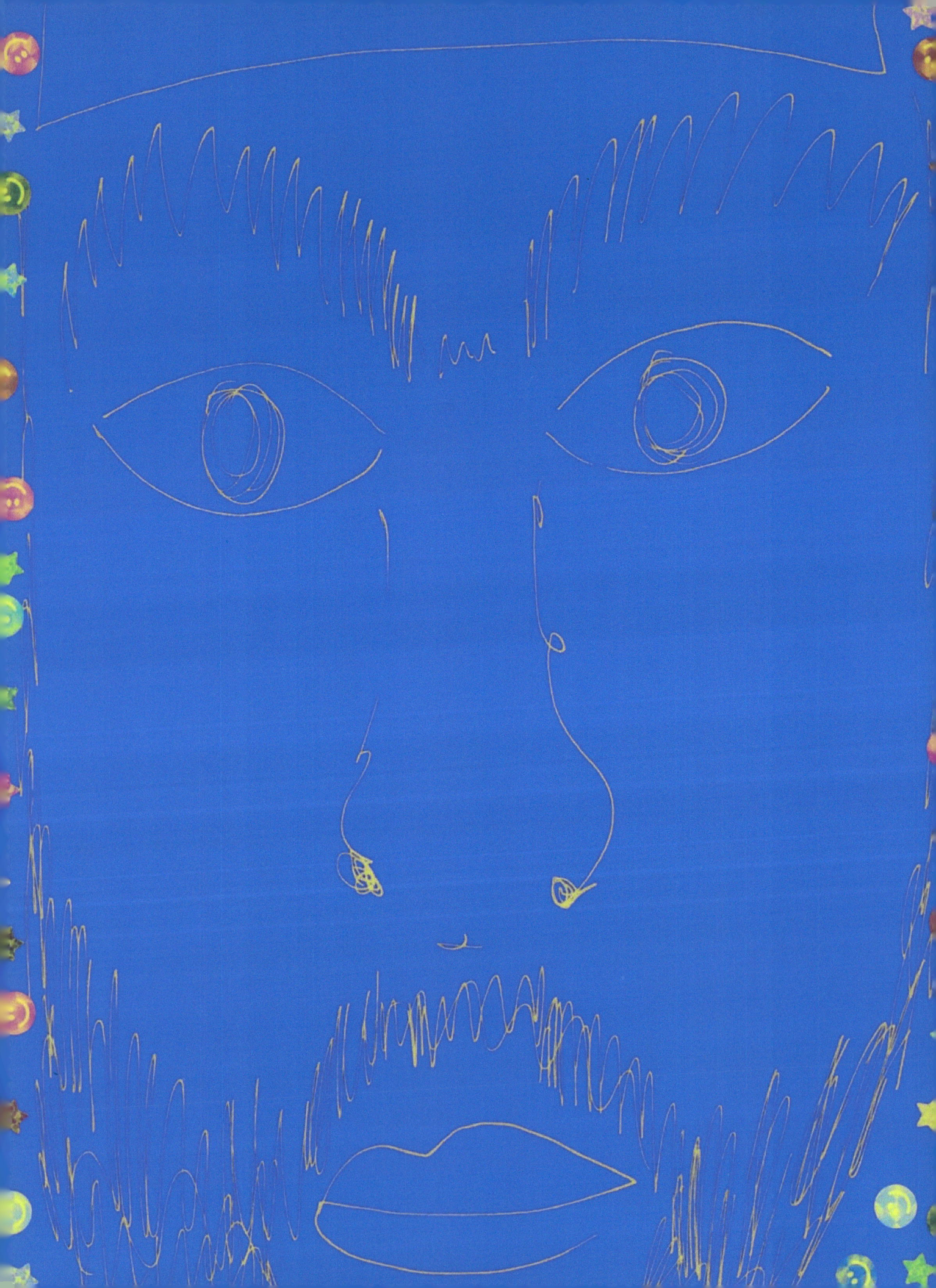

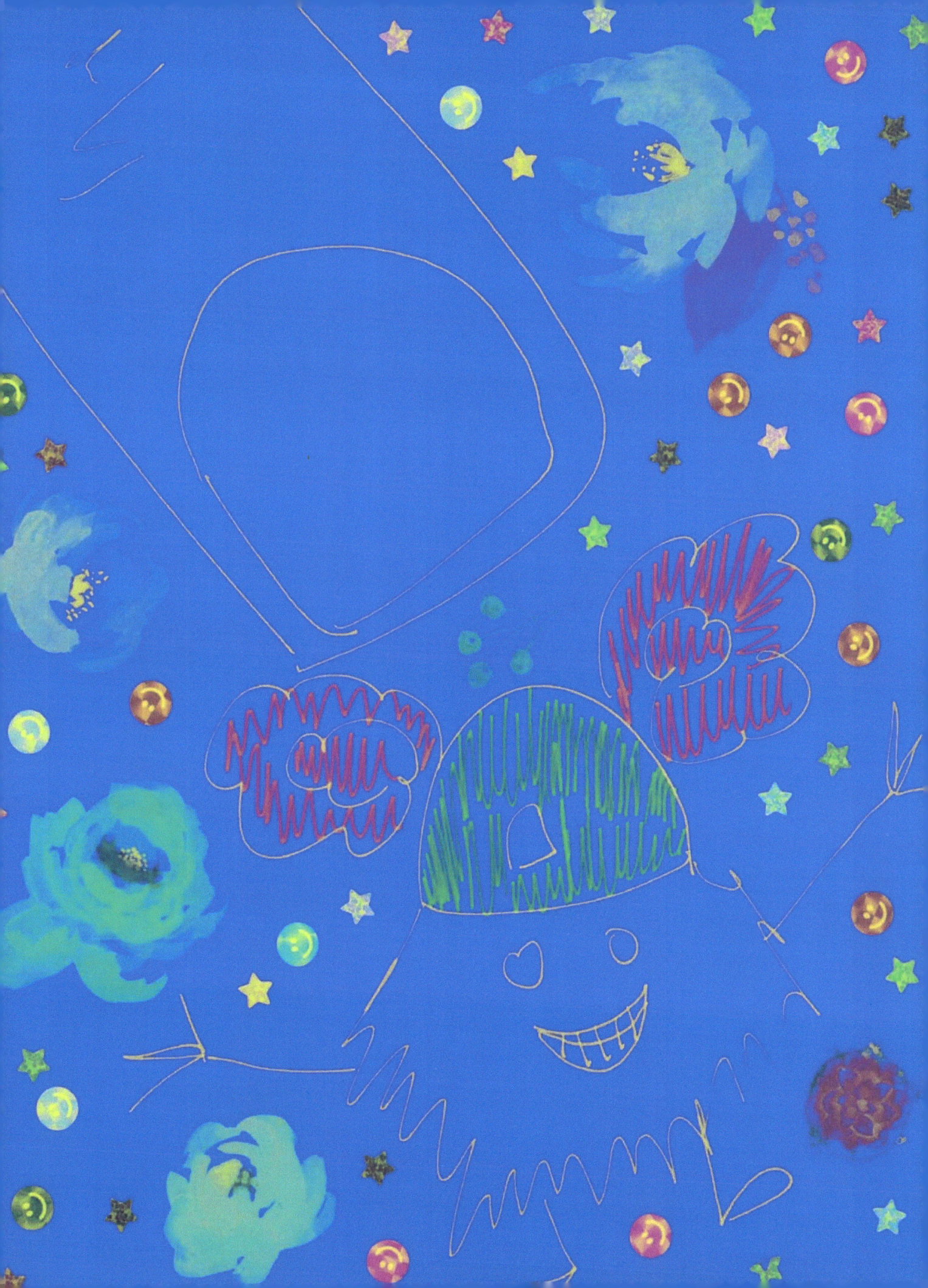

Juan didn't get it,
But he acted like he did.
But Fear was like, really smart.
And he totally knew Juan didn't get it.
So Fear laughed out loud.

Fear's laugh wasn't a pretty laugh. Nope! It definitely was not!

It was more like, one of those laughs that you hear in the dark when there's no one around to laugh about it.

Yeah, like one of those laughs.

After he laughed,
Fear looked at Juan's face.
And he totally knew Juan didn't like his laugh.
So Fear got suddenly very serious.
Almost angry,
but like, not angry yet.

What do you feel when I laugh? Fear asked Juan. Juan didn't really know what to do.

Because Juan was alone.

Juan realized that Fear's anger was only getting bigger and bigger. Tell me what did you feel when I laughed? Fear yelled at Juan. So Juan answered.

Because Juan was alone.

It feels dark and it's loud. It sounds like screams. It's scary and you can't see anyone around you. You cant even see Anger to play in your team. And you don't even know where you are, but you are not in a pretty place.

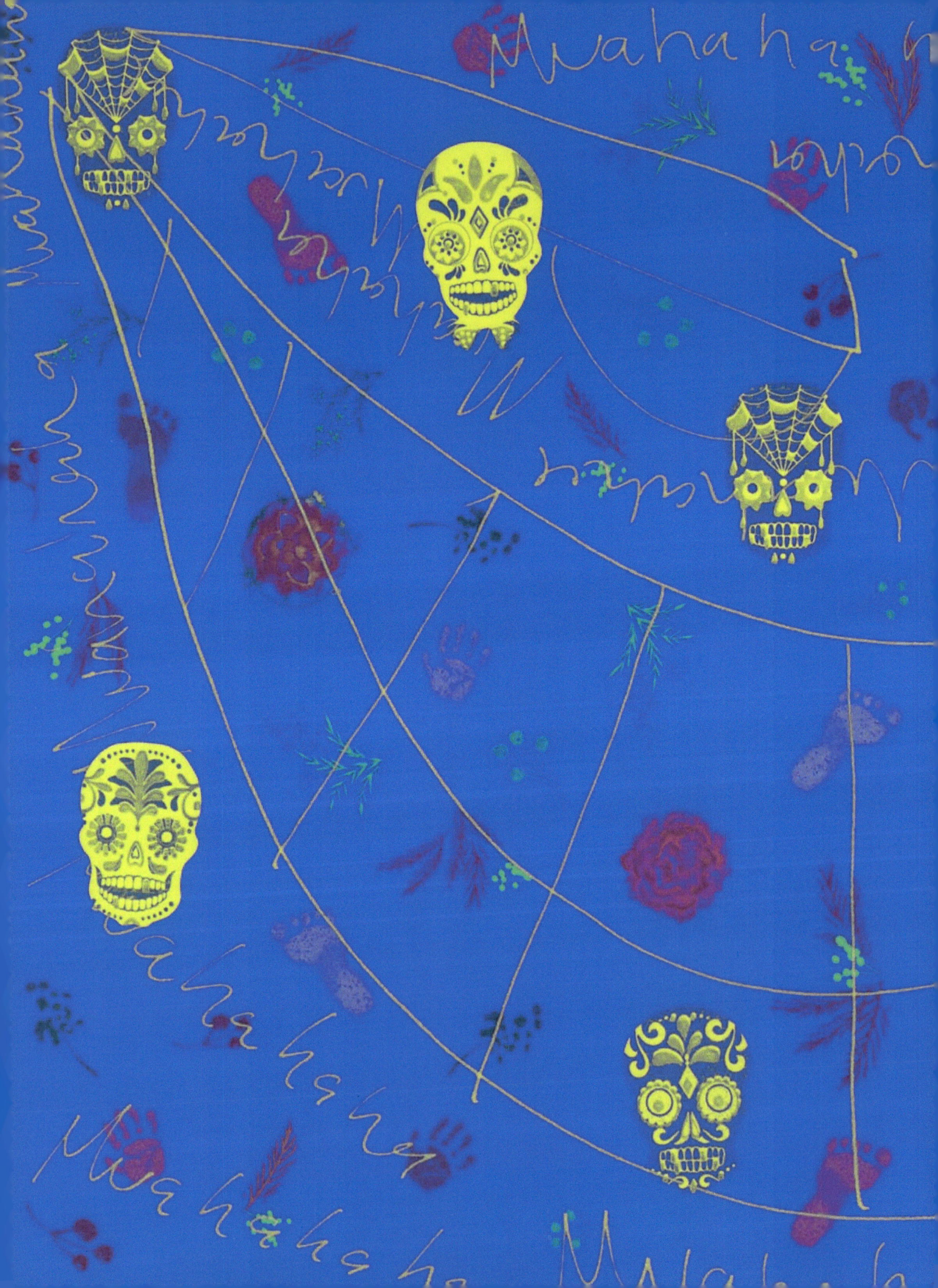

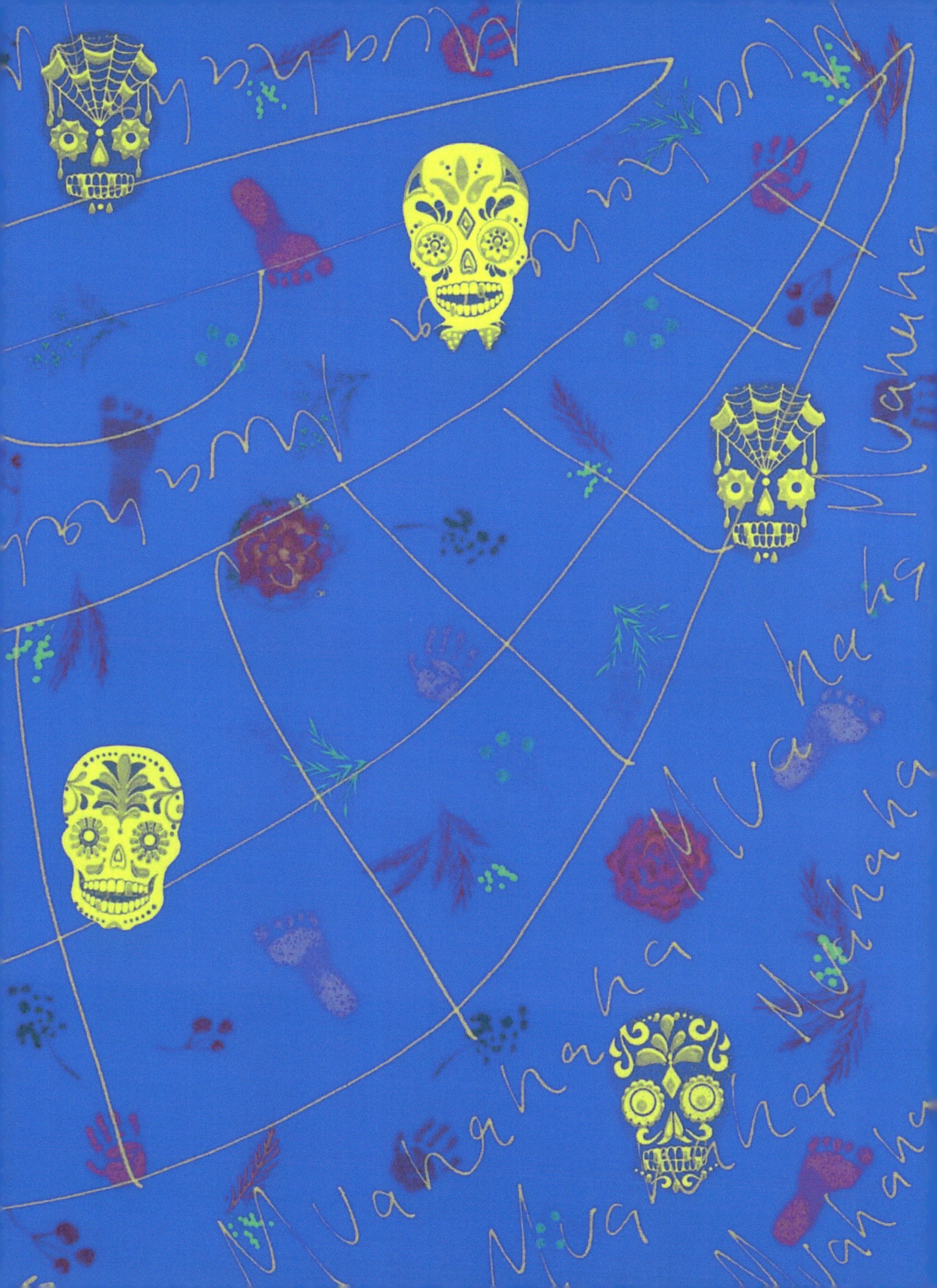

And you close your eyes hoping that the screams would stop.
But it only makes it worse.
So you open your eyes again.
And as Juan opened his eyes, Juan saw that Fear was angry.

And Fear wasn't a little something in the distance anymore. Now Fear was all Anger. And Anger is very very very big, and it only gets bigger and bigger. And Anger says no words. Anger only observes and It doesn't let anyone notice him.

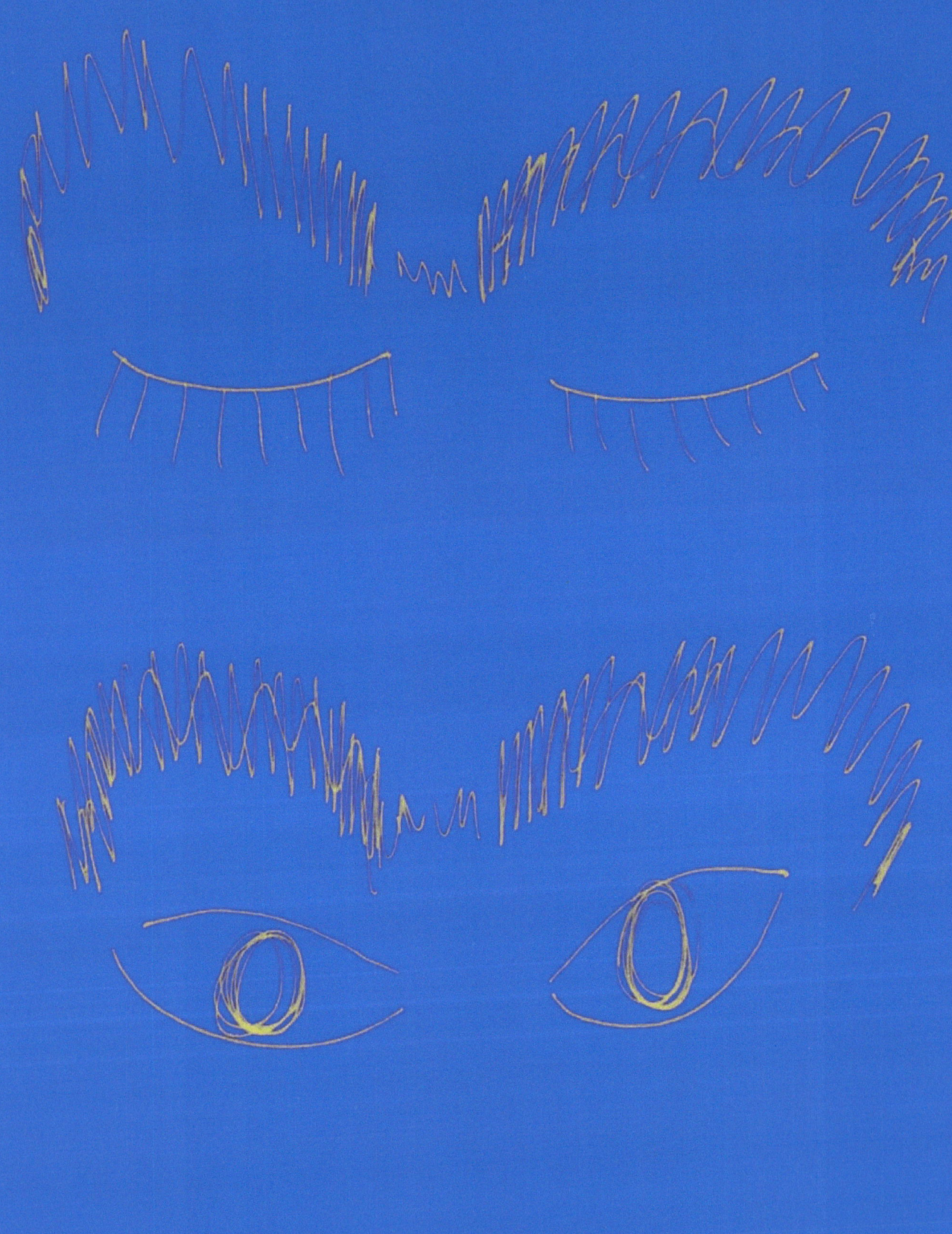

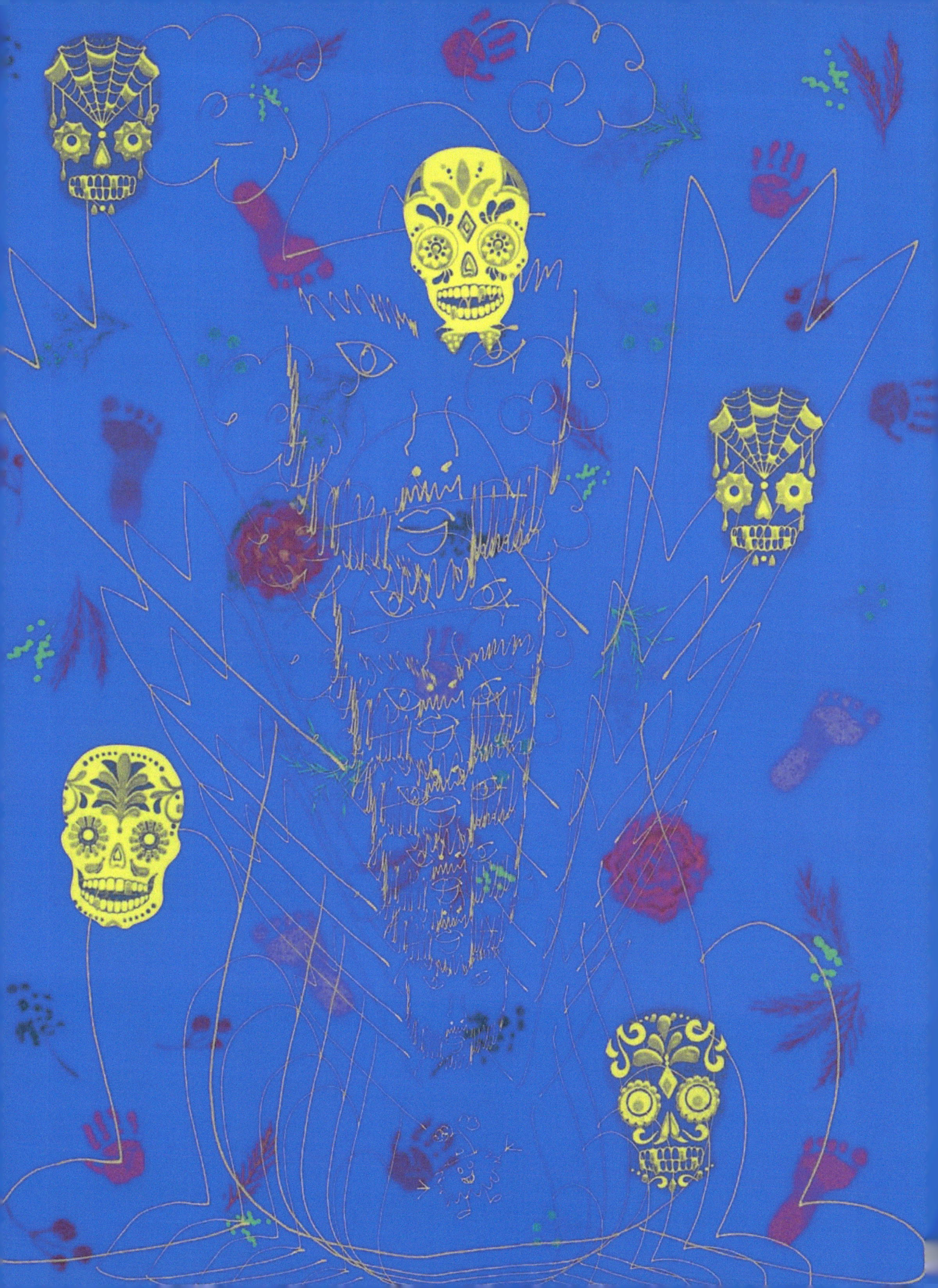

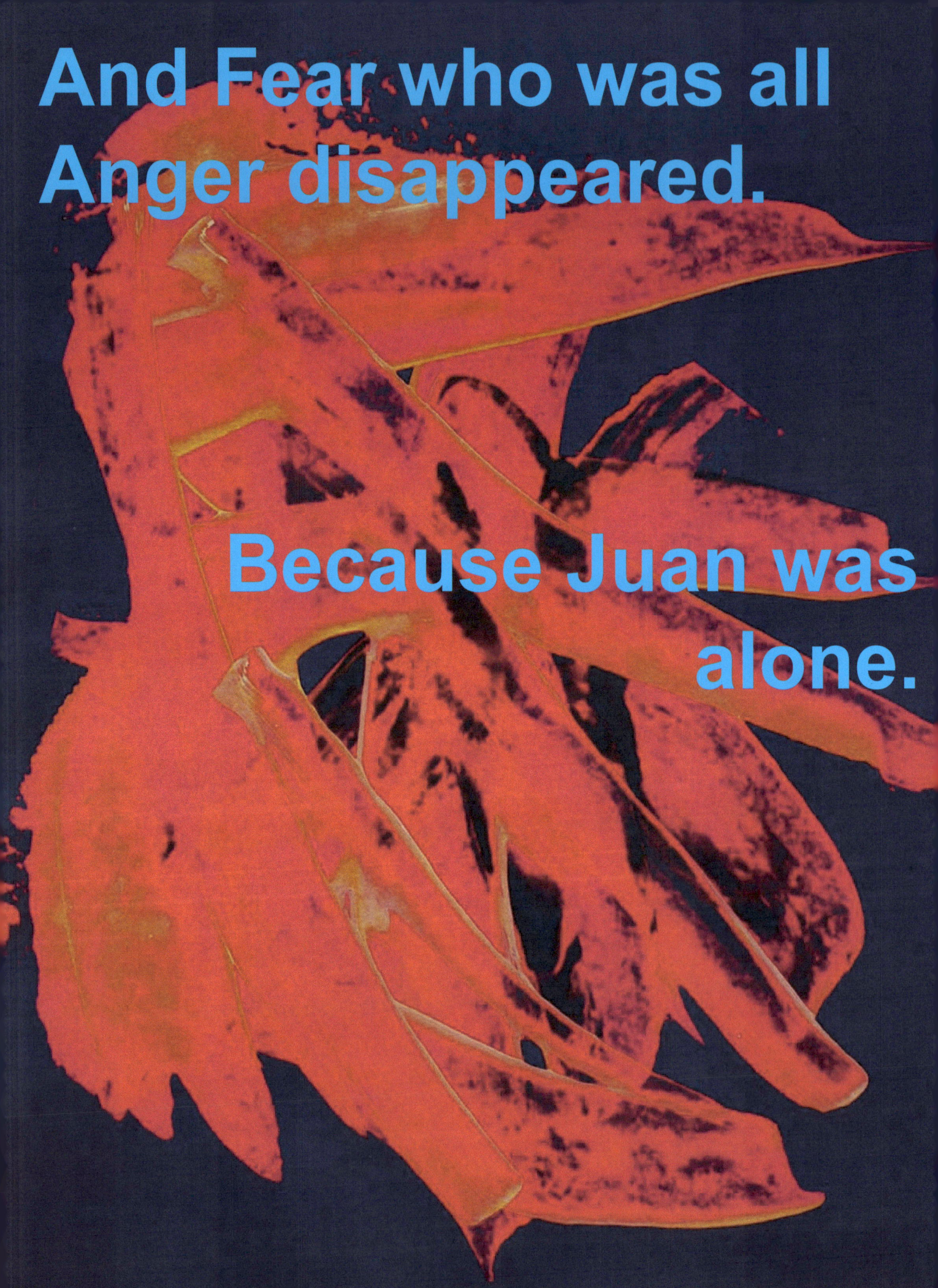

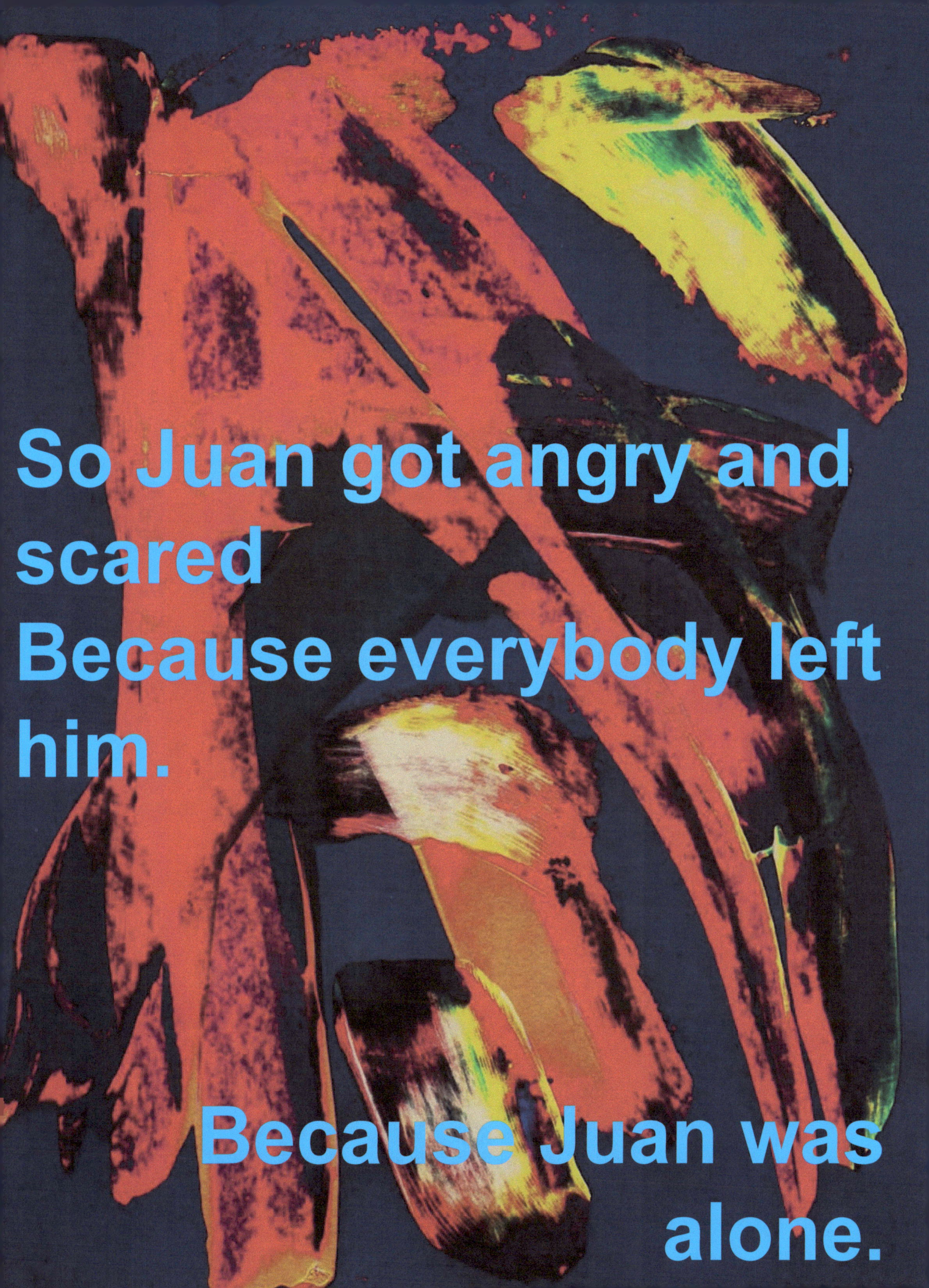

And Juan went looking for Fear who was all Anger.

In the dark, Juan wandered and wandered. He wandered a lot.

But Juan couldn't seem to notice Fear who was all Anger.

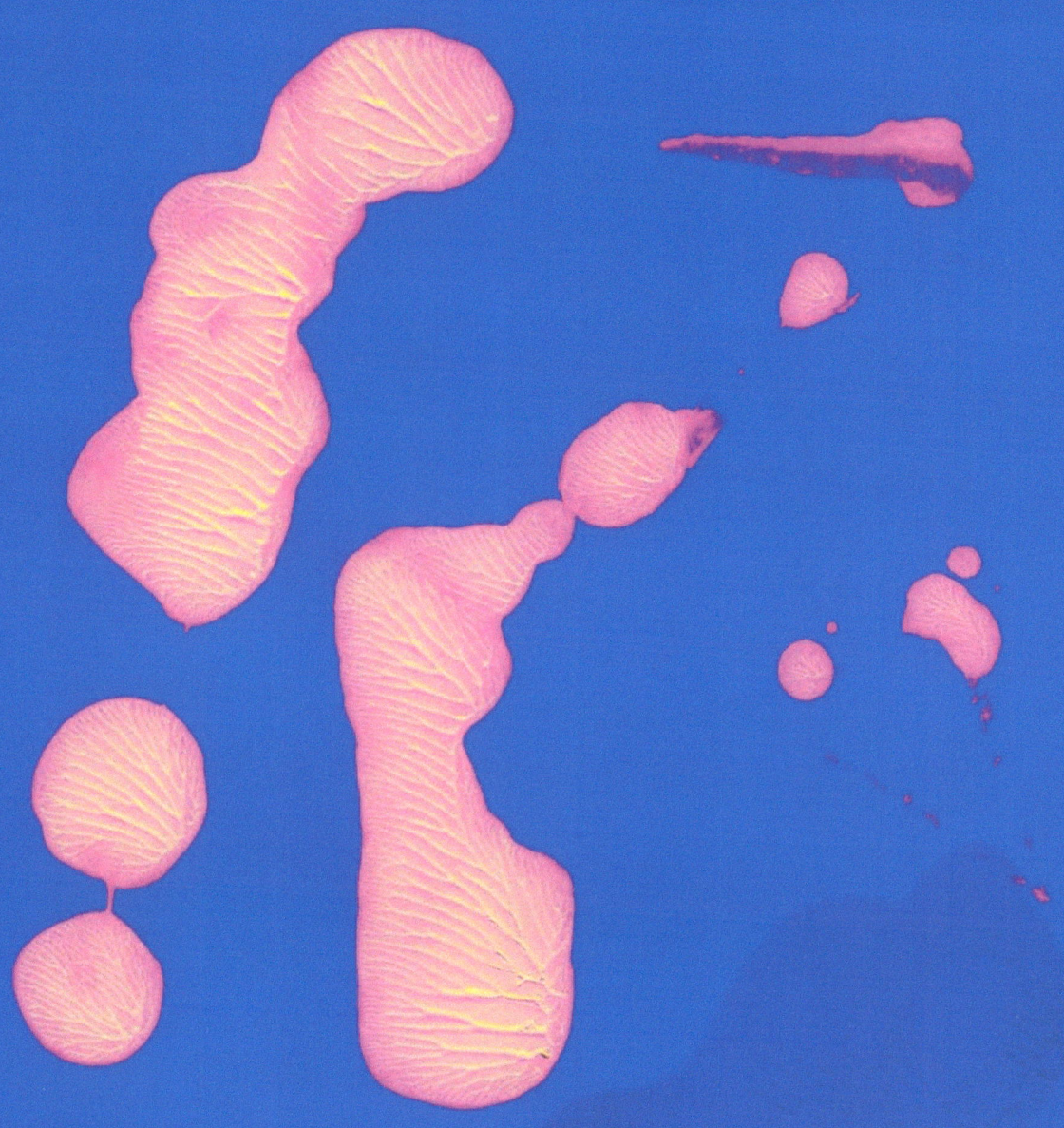

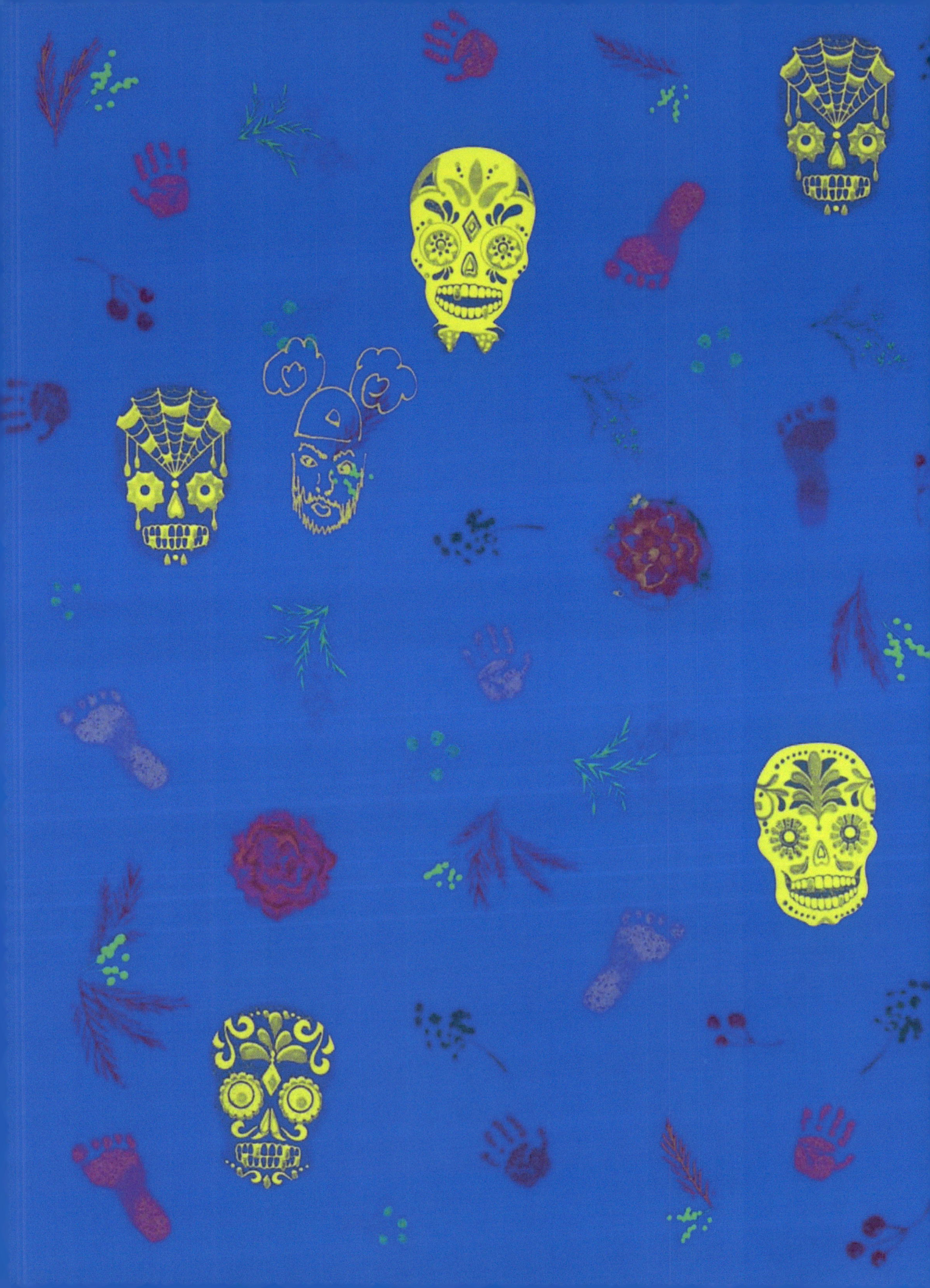

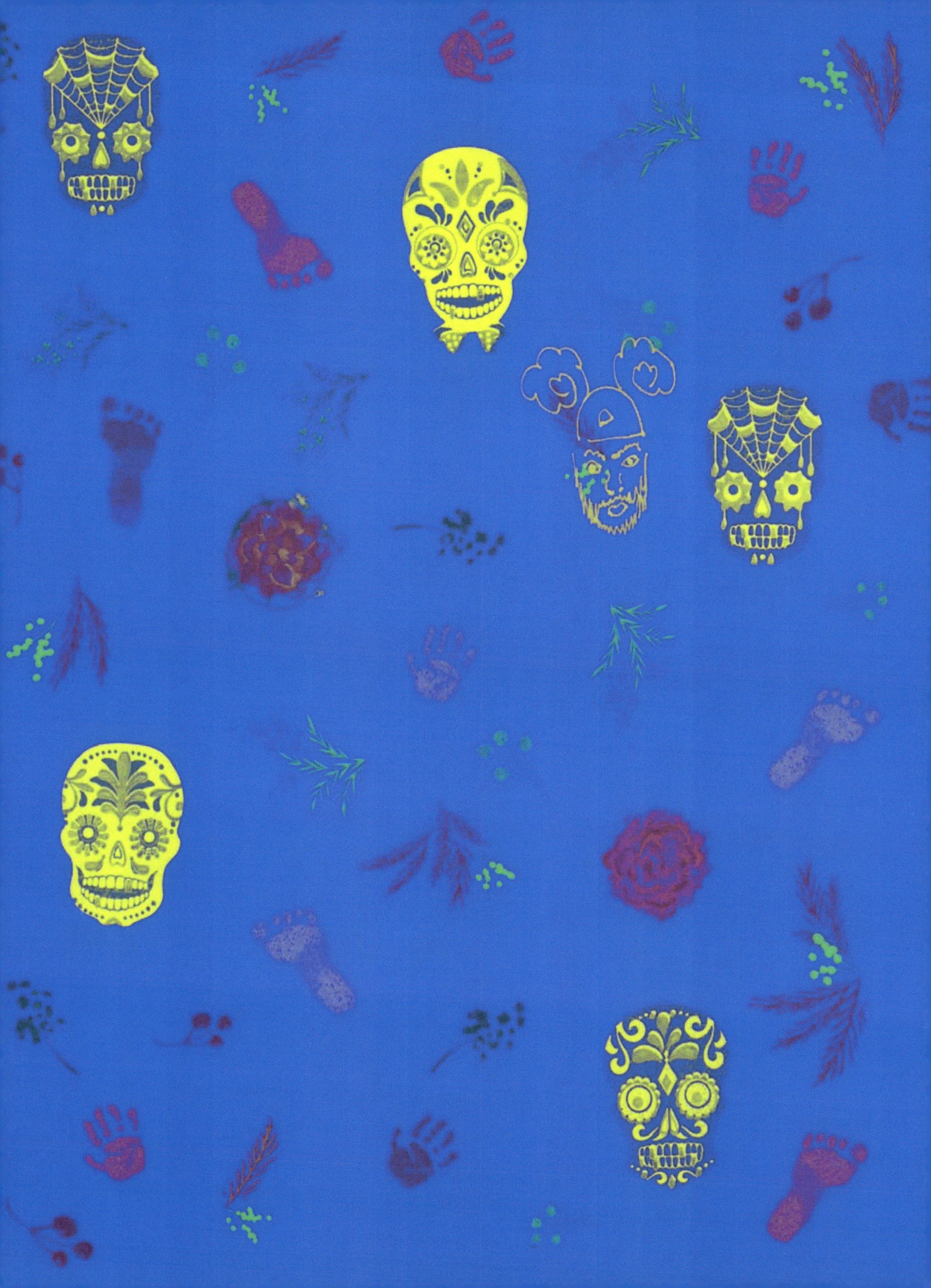

In the dark, someone heard a little something in the distance.

And someone saw that it was Juan.

Because Juan was alone.

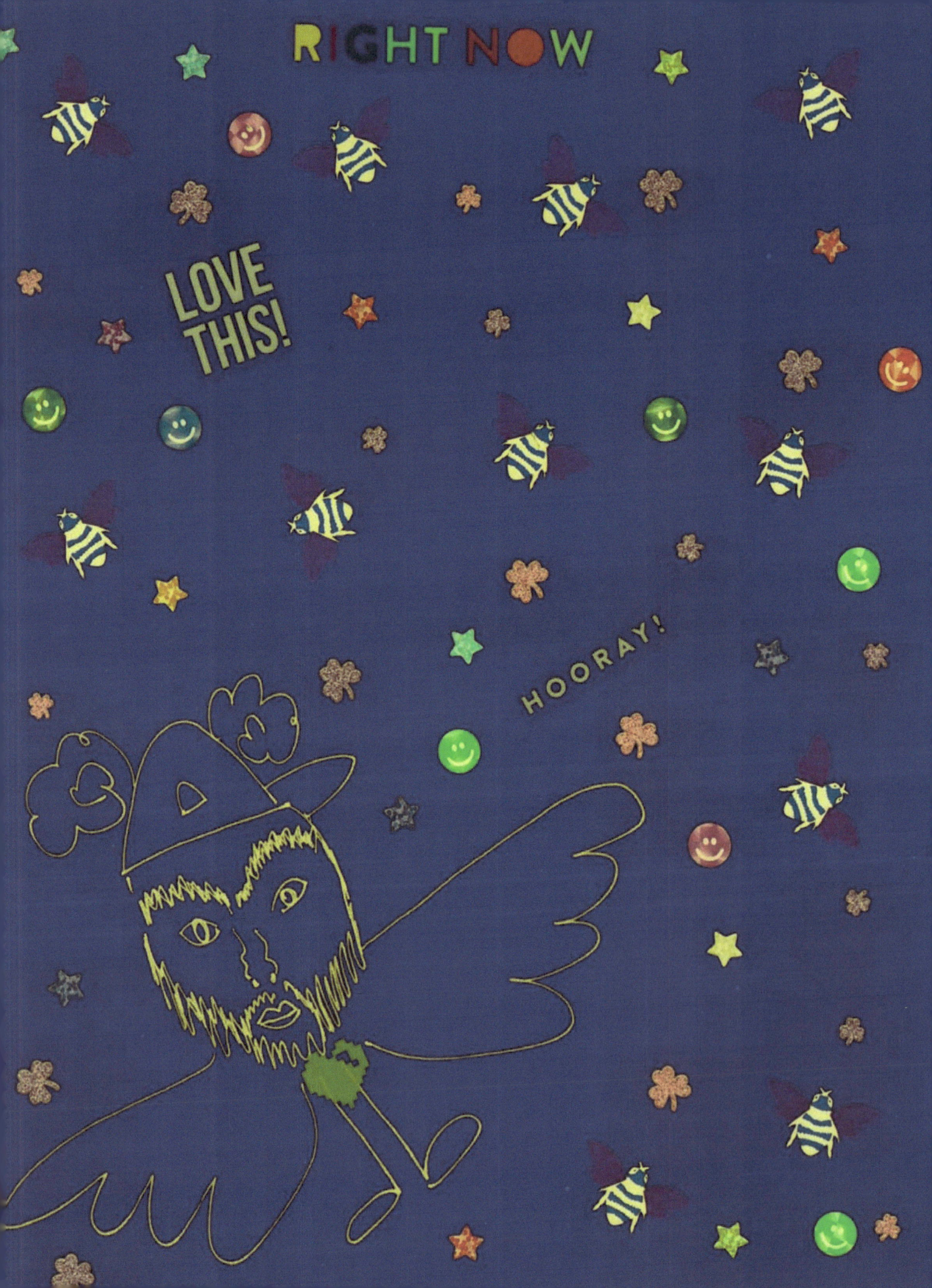

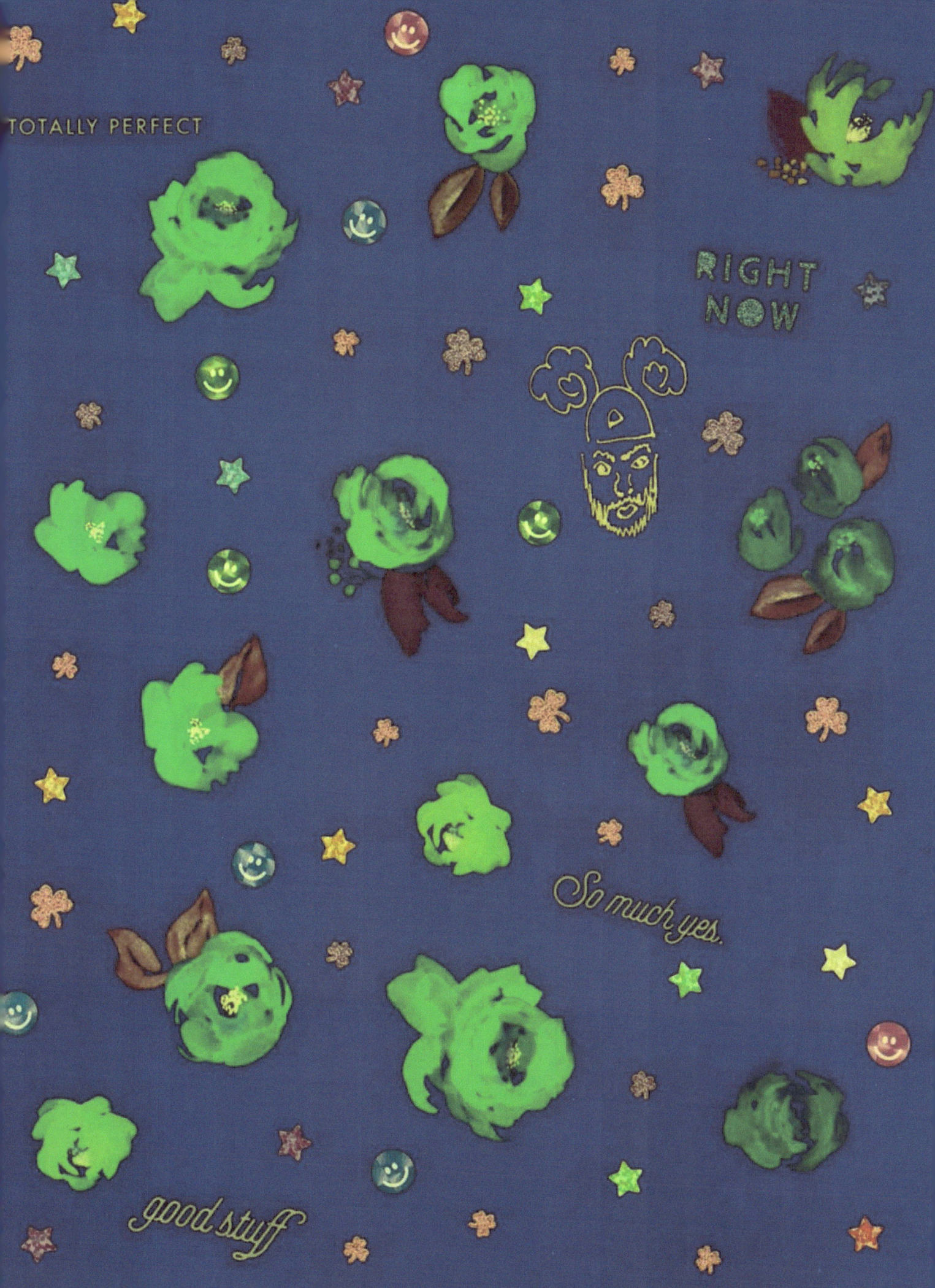

And someone got closer to Juan.
And someone talked to Juan.
And someone asked Juan what he was doing.

Why are you in the dark? And why are you angry and scared? Someone asked Juan.

Someone said,
It seems that,
In the dark,
you have wandered
and wandered.
You have wandered
a lot.

Are you lost?
Are you staying here
in the dark?

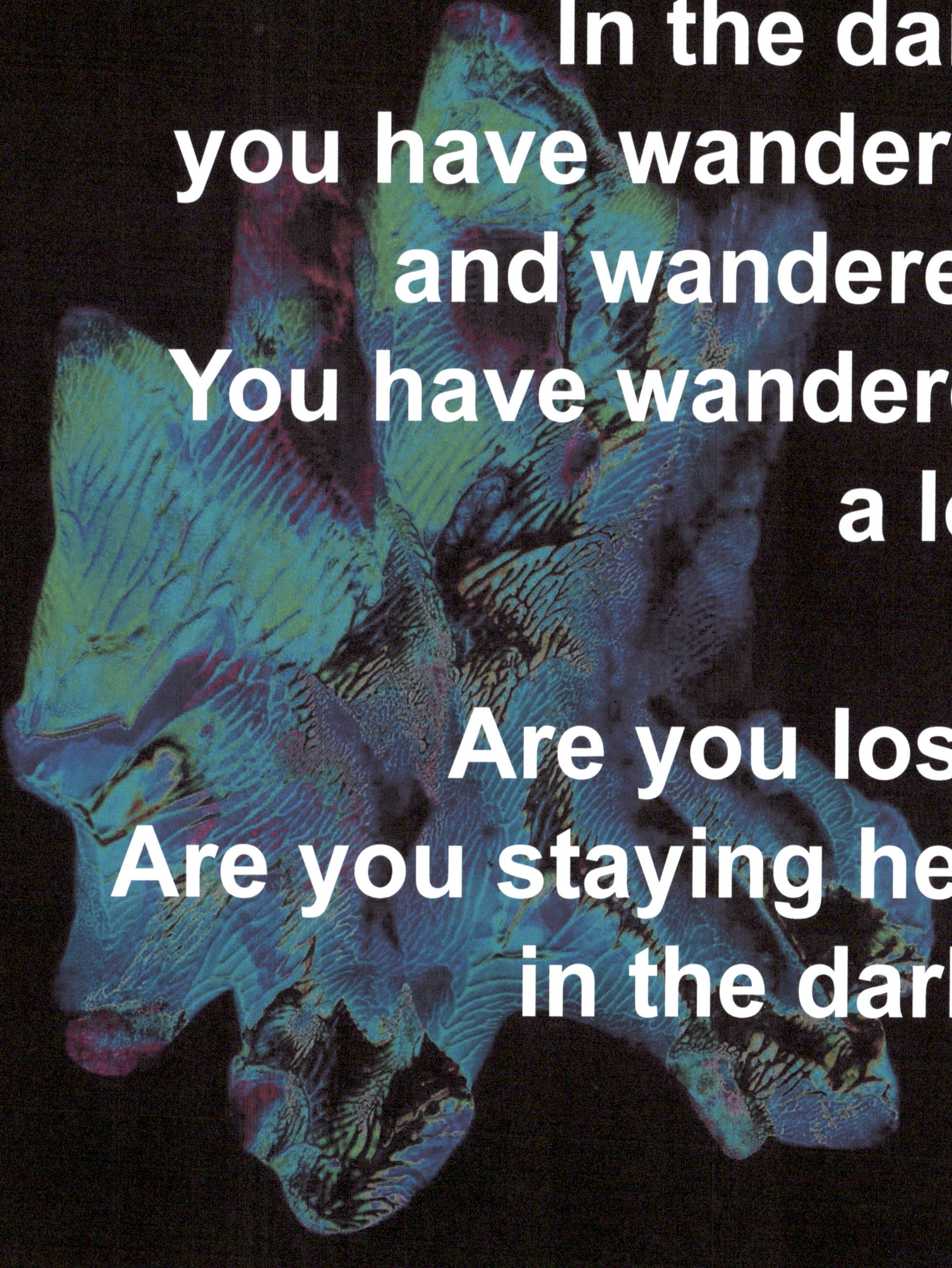

Juan looked at someone. Someone seemed like a nice guy. Like those guys who would help you find your way back home, if you ever get lost. So Juan answered someone.

Because Juan was alone.

I guess I am lost. And I really don't want to stay here in the dark angry and scared, but I'm looking for something. Something my parents can't give me. And you see, my mother is the Earth and my father is the Sun.

And like, they gave me everything, literally everything. But somehow everything wasn't enough. And you see, someone. You seem like a nice guy. Like those guys who would help you find your way back home, if you ever get lost.

But I can't go back home yet. Not without that something. And, to tell you the truth, I don't know what that something is. But I can't go back home yet. Cause you see, I'm angry and scared. But I don't have that something yet.

And someone saw something in Juan's eyes.
It wasn't Anger what he saw, nor Fear.
Someone saw himself in Juan's eyes.
Because, like, you know, if you just get very close to someone, like really close.

You can totally see your reflection on their eyes.
And, like, that's what someone saw.
Someone saw his reflection on Juan.
And someone liked it.

Because reflections are totally cool.

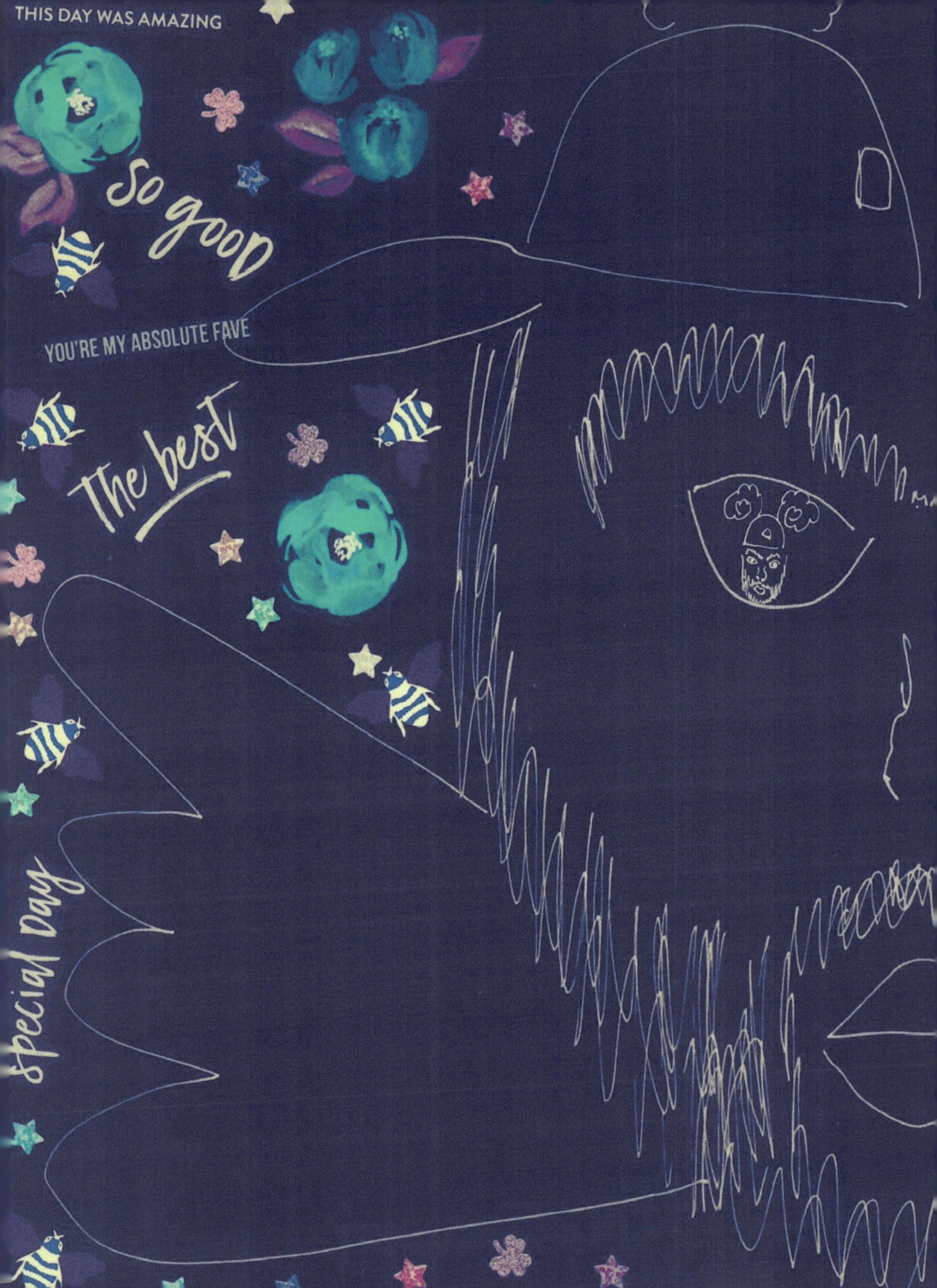

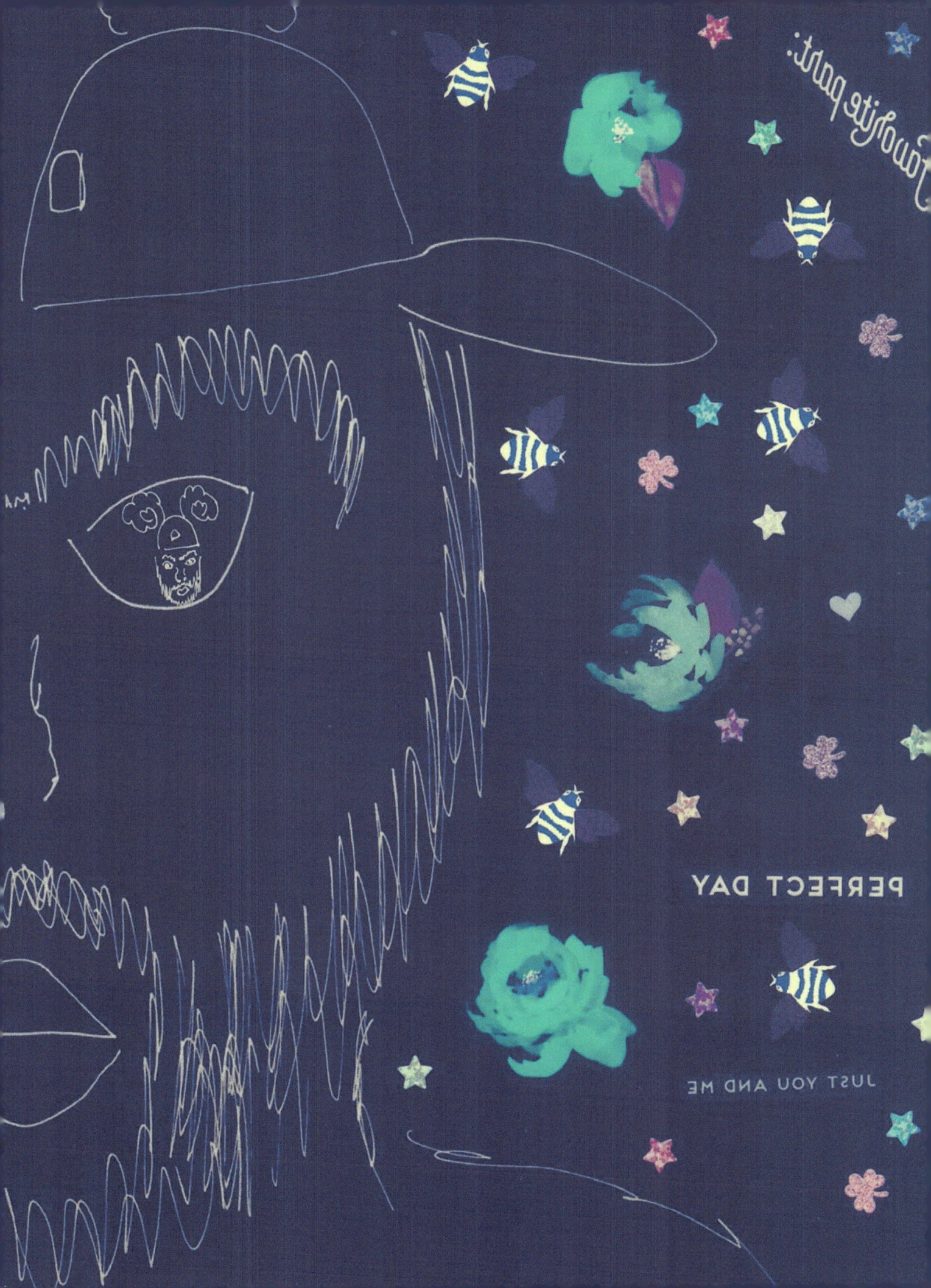

So someone said to Juan.
Yo, you know what?
I totally like you.
Cause like, I can totally see myself in you.
And you see, I am a nice guy. Like those guys who would help you find your way back home, if you ever get lost.

That's totally me.
I'm totally that guy.
I am that someone.

So Juan really liked someone.
Especially after someone said that.

Juan was totally in like with this someone.

At this point Juan totally felt like they were buddies.
Like those buddies that can ask each other for help, and favors, and all those kind of stuff. Like whatever.

So at this point Juan had to ask who this someone was.

Because if they were friends, and they were so similar.
Like, we need to know someone's name.

We cannot keep calling someone, someone.

After a while it's just awkward to call someone, someone.

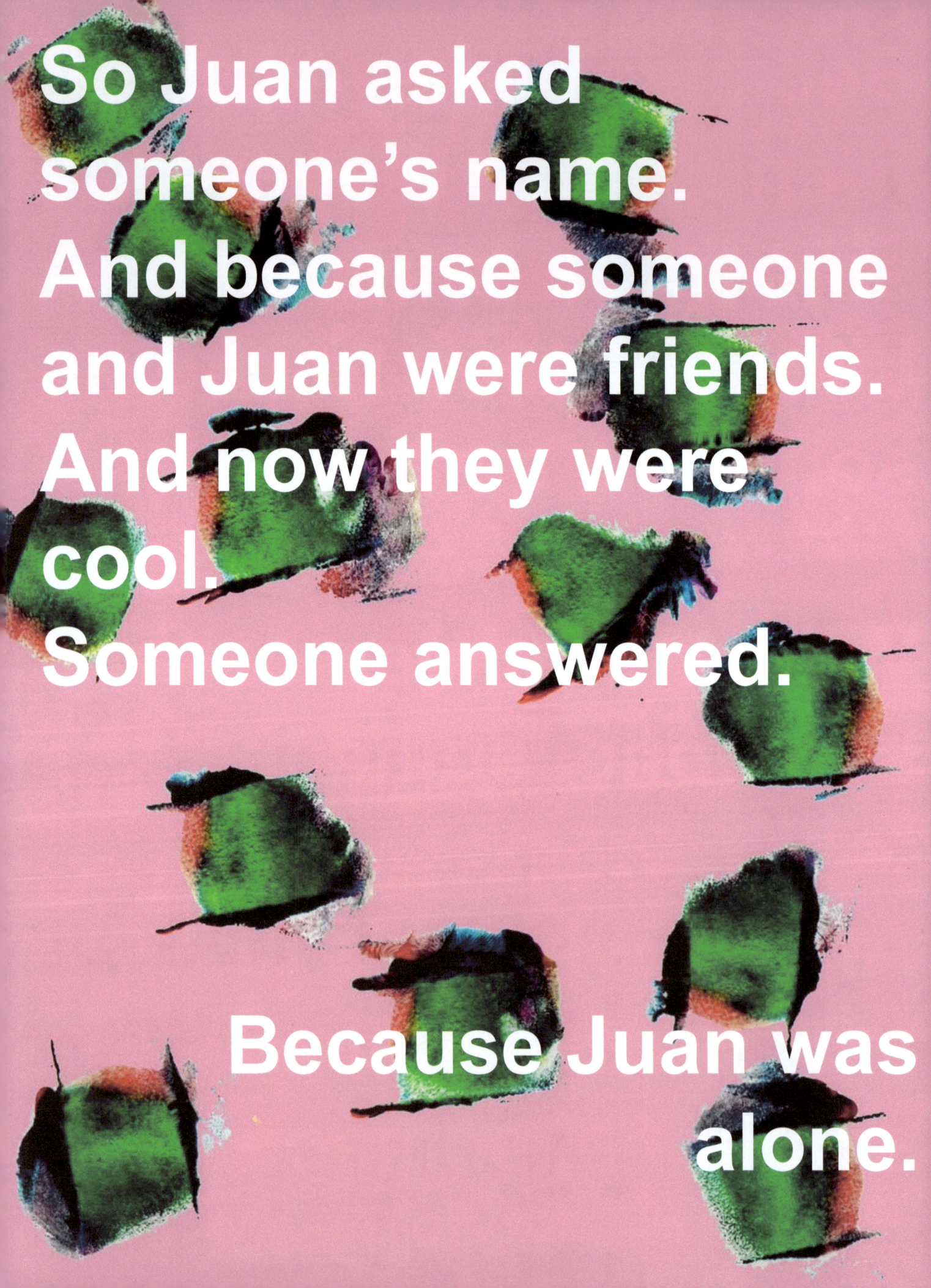

So Juan asked someone's name.
And because someone and Juan were friends.
And now they were cool.
Someone answered.

Because Juan was alone.

I am Hope, my name is Hope. And you see, I'm a nice guy. Like those guys who would help you find your way back home, if you ever get lost. And I will help you find that something. Cause I'm a nice guy. And that's what nice guys do.

And as someone, who was Hope because it was like his name, said that to Juan.

Hope disappeared in front of Juan's eyes!

Because Juan was alone, don't you forget!

Juan couldn't believe Hope had disappeared! And then, Juan realized something. Something that we totally missed. Hope had not left! Hope is in Juan's eyes. Because that's where he disappeared. In front of his eyes, duh!

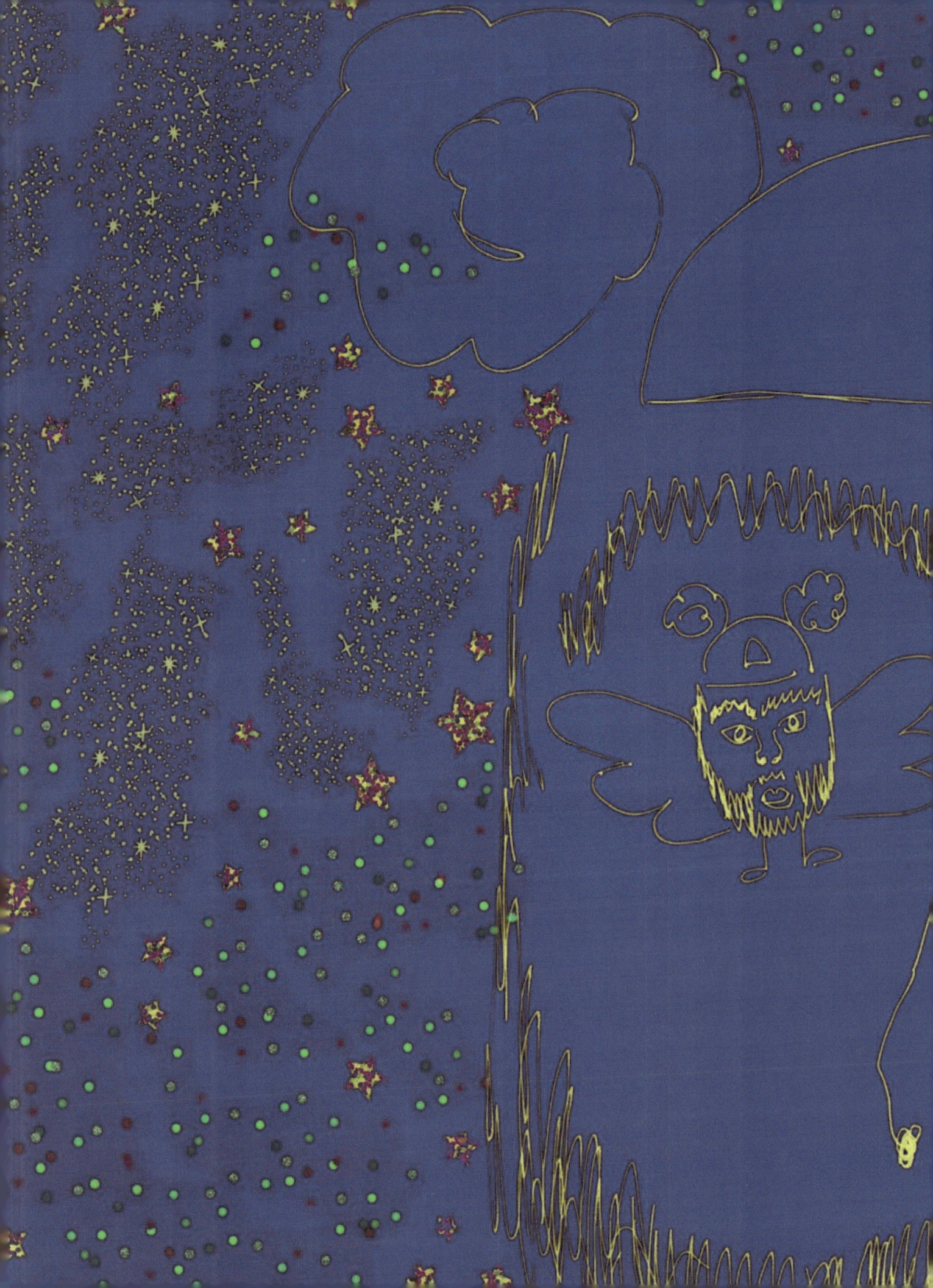

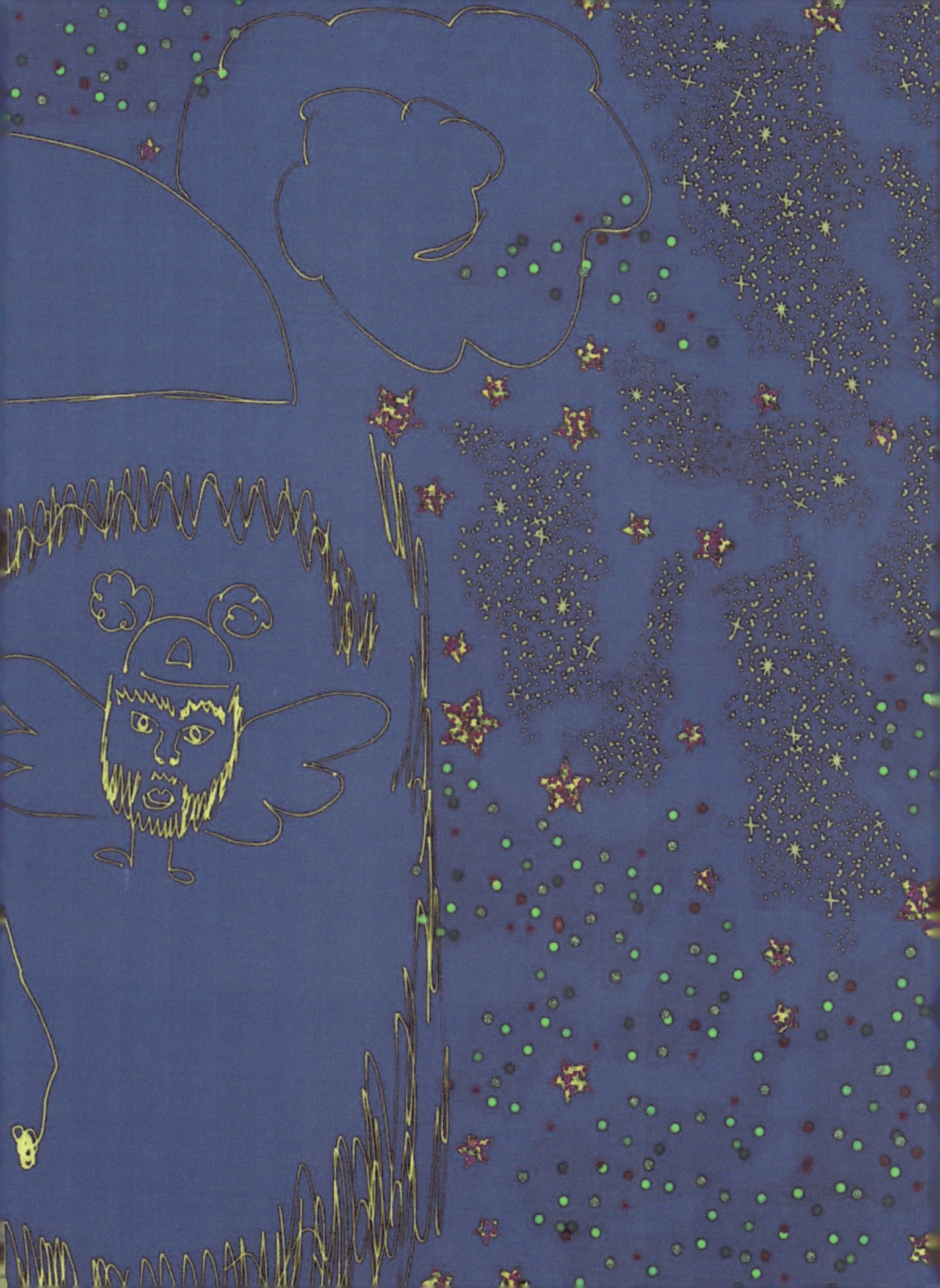

So don't worry about Hope. Hope is fine.

By the way, did I mention that Hope is a badass? Because Hope is.
So if Hope is a badass and Hope is in Juan's eyes...
Then Juan is a badass too. Duh!

It's very simple, like so simple. So Juan the badass went looking for that something that he didn't know what it was, but it was something that his parents couldn't give him. Remember? The reason this badass story started.

But what could that something be?
Juan thought.
If I don't know what it looks like. How can I find it?
Even with Hope in my eyes it's going to be hard to find that something.

Man, I'm lost. Juan thought.

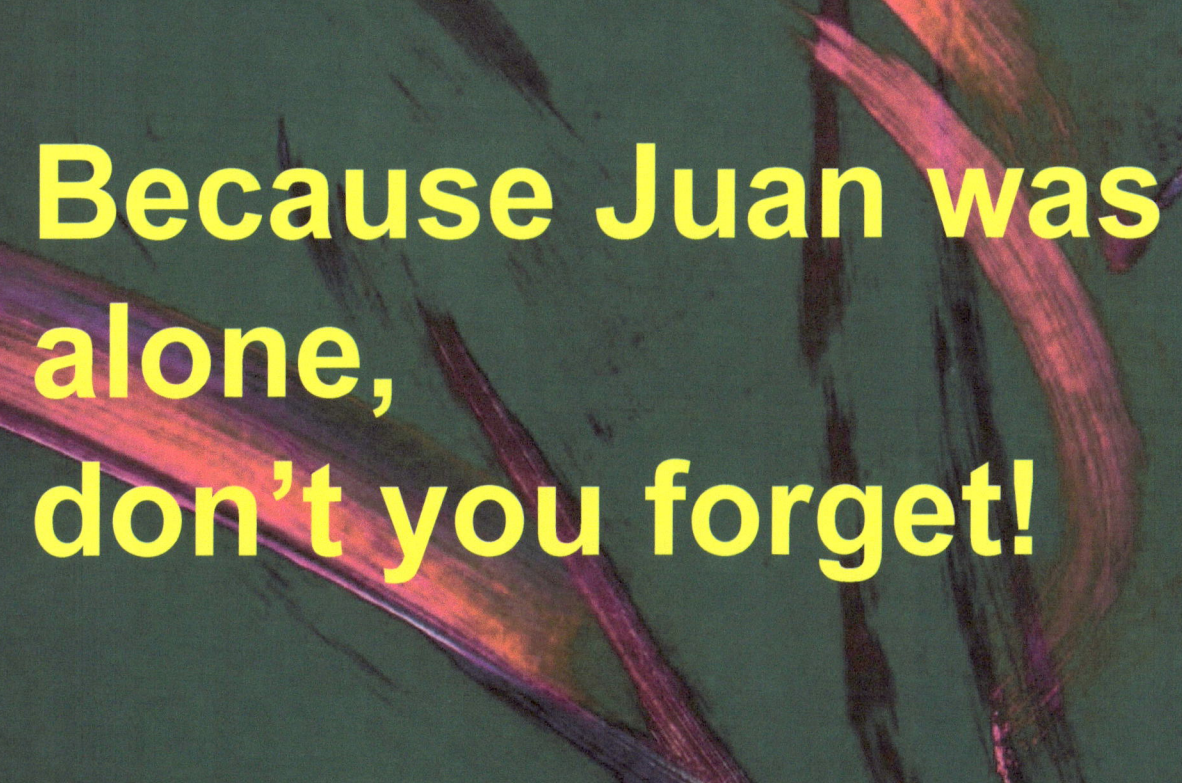

Actually forget about it. Lets make it easier for Juan. What if we can be totally cool with him?

Lets change the story a bit before we all get bored, Close this book, And go to bed.

Lets say we give poor freaking Juan that something.

And before this story gets way too complicated to keep up with. Lets give that something a name.

So we don't know what this something looks like, but we have to believe it exists

because we are like, looking for it.

We went through all this trouble for this something, right?

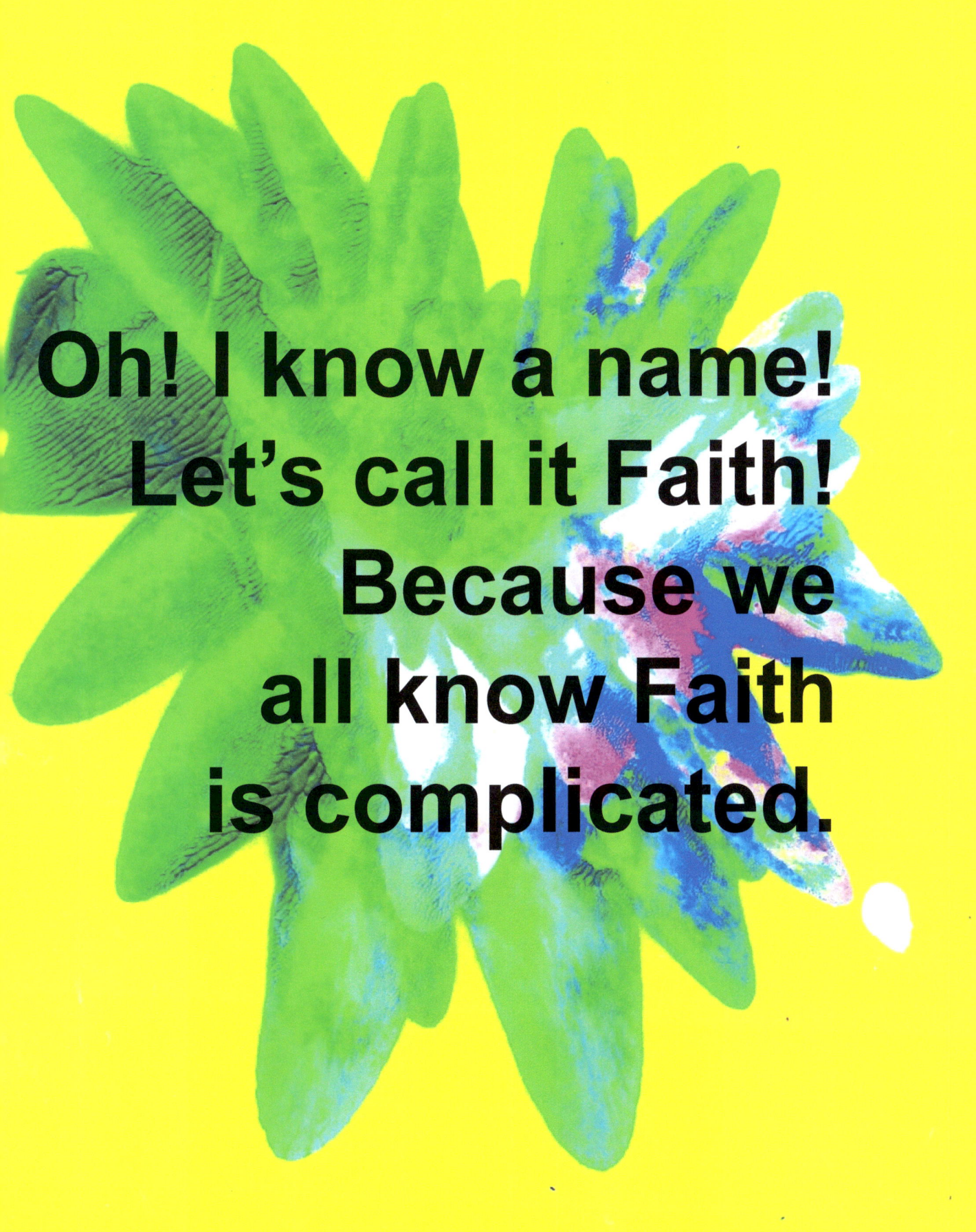

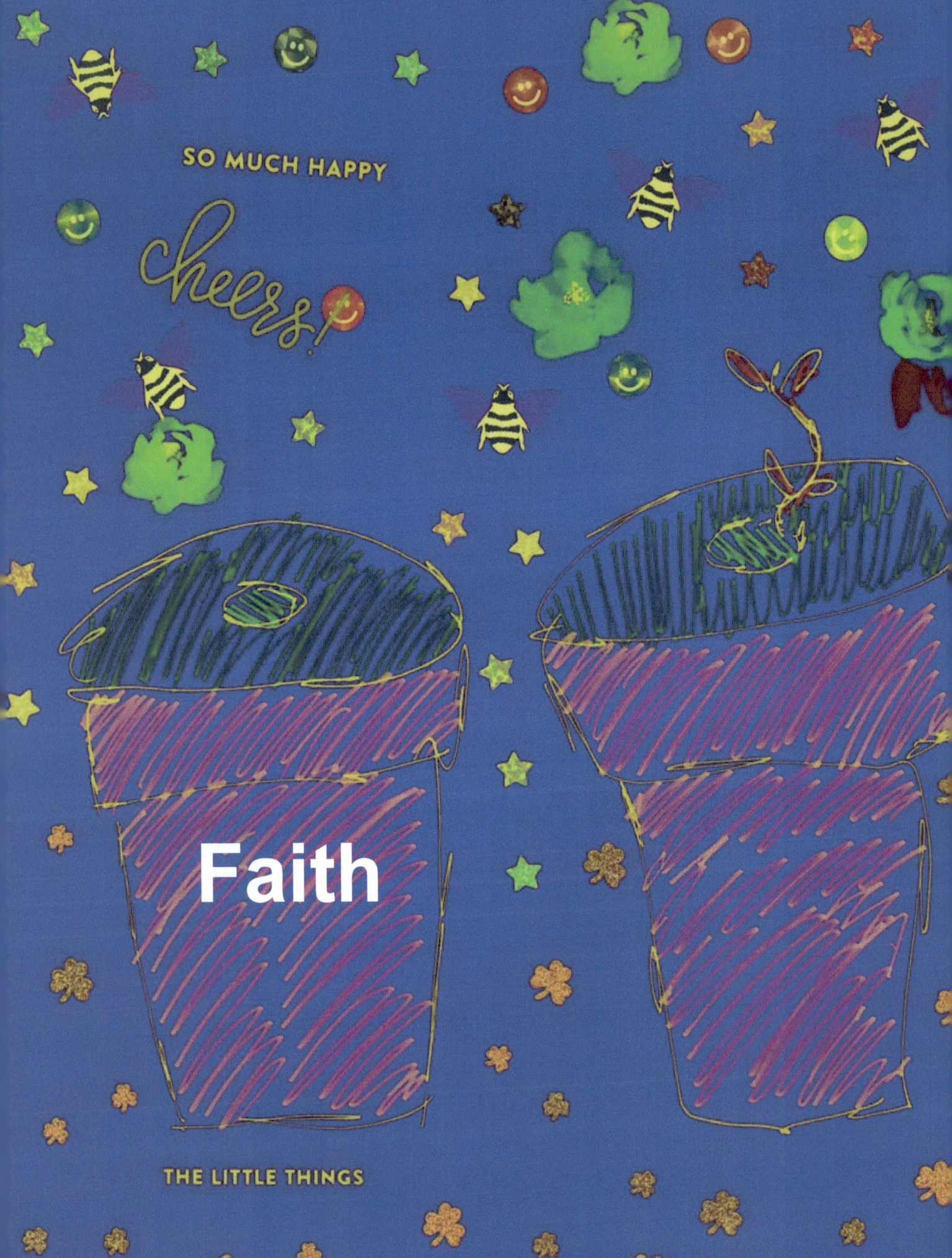

Faith

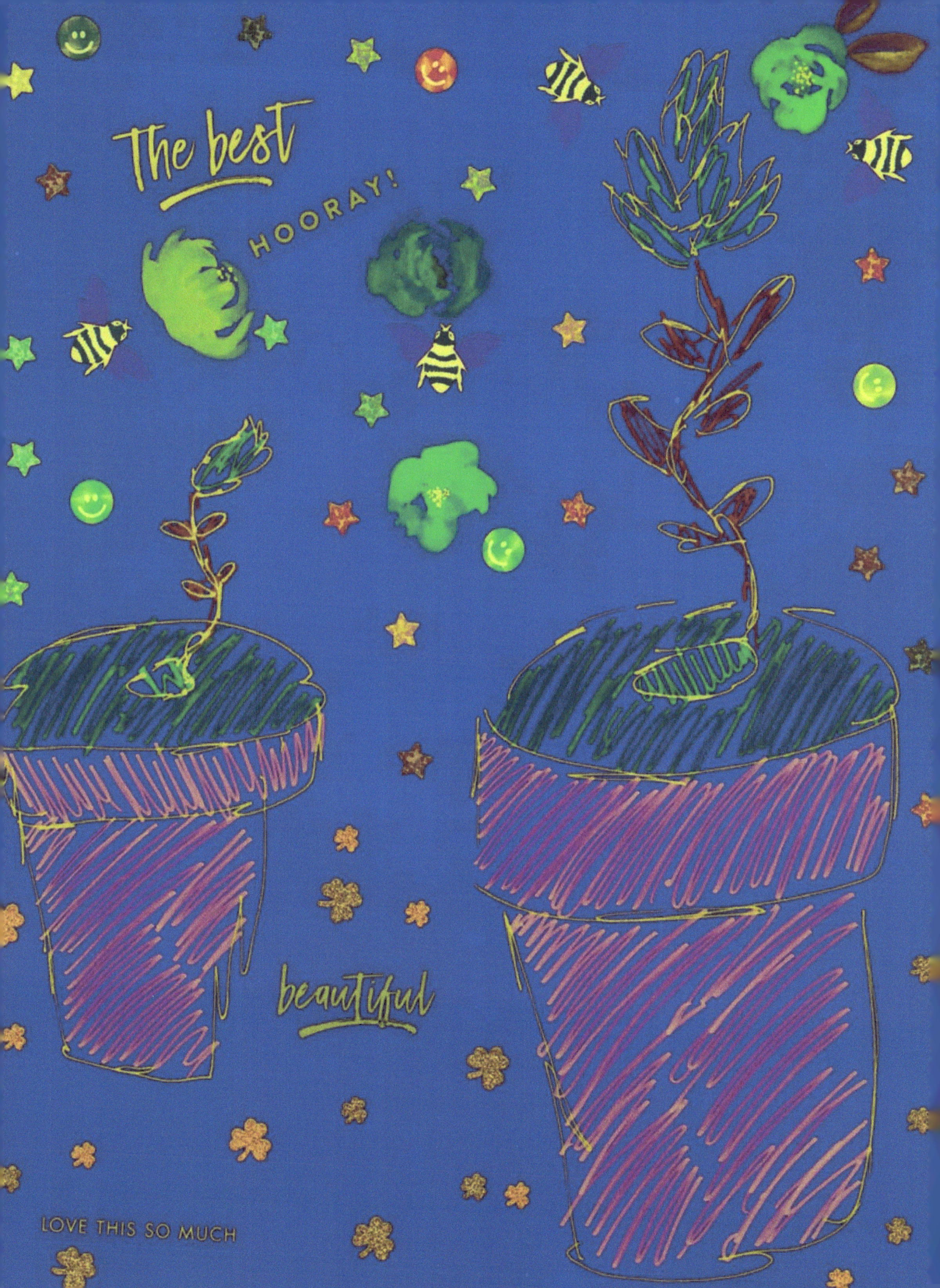

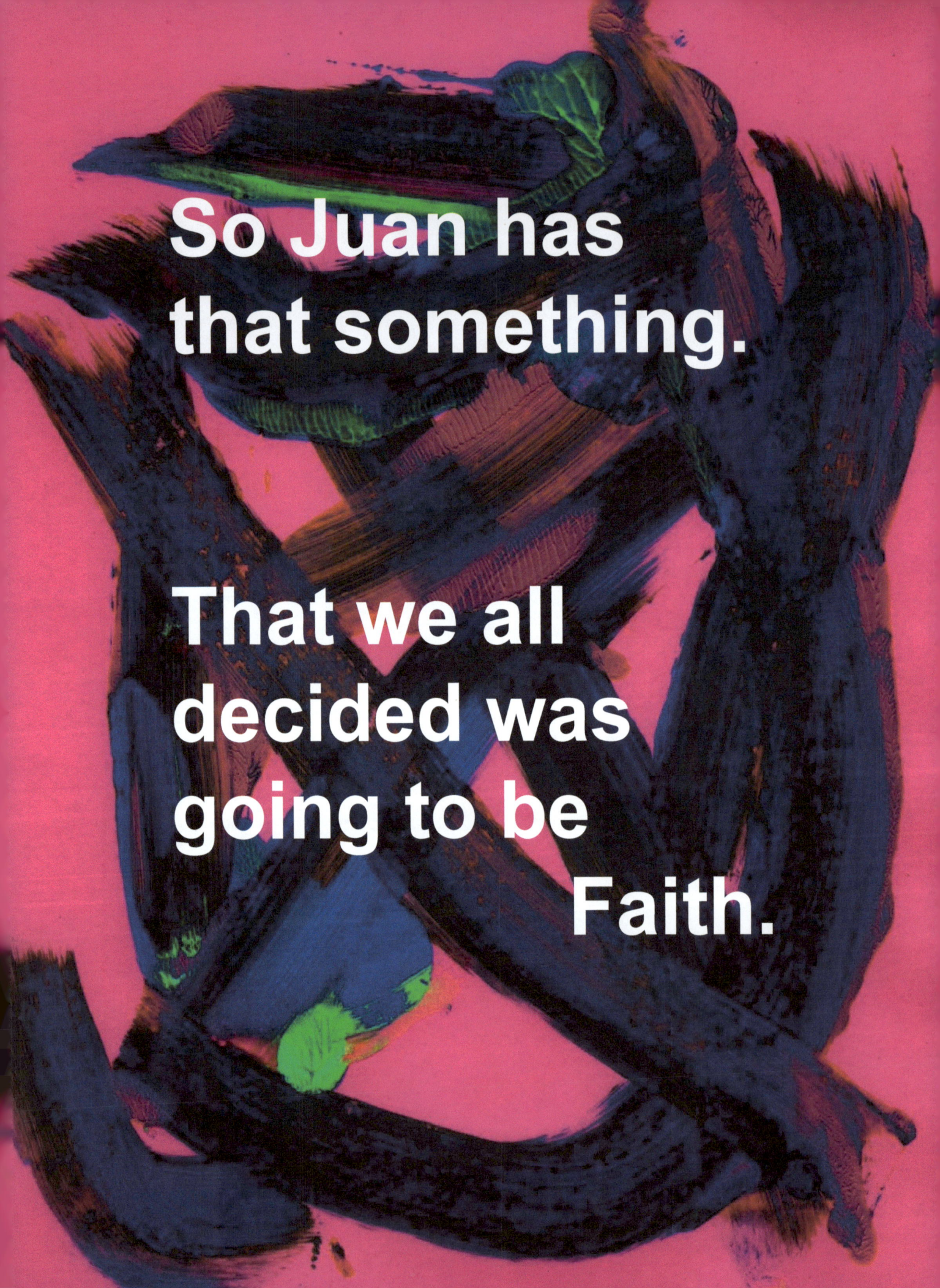

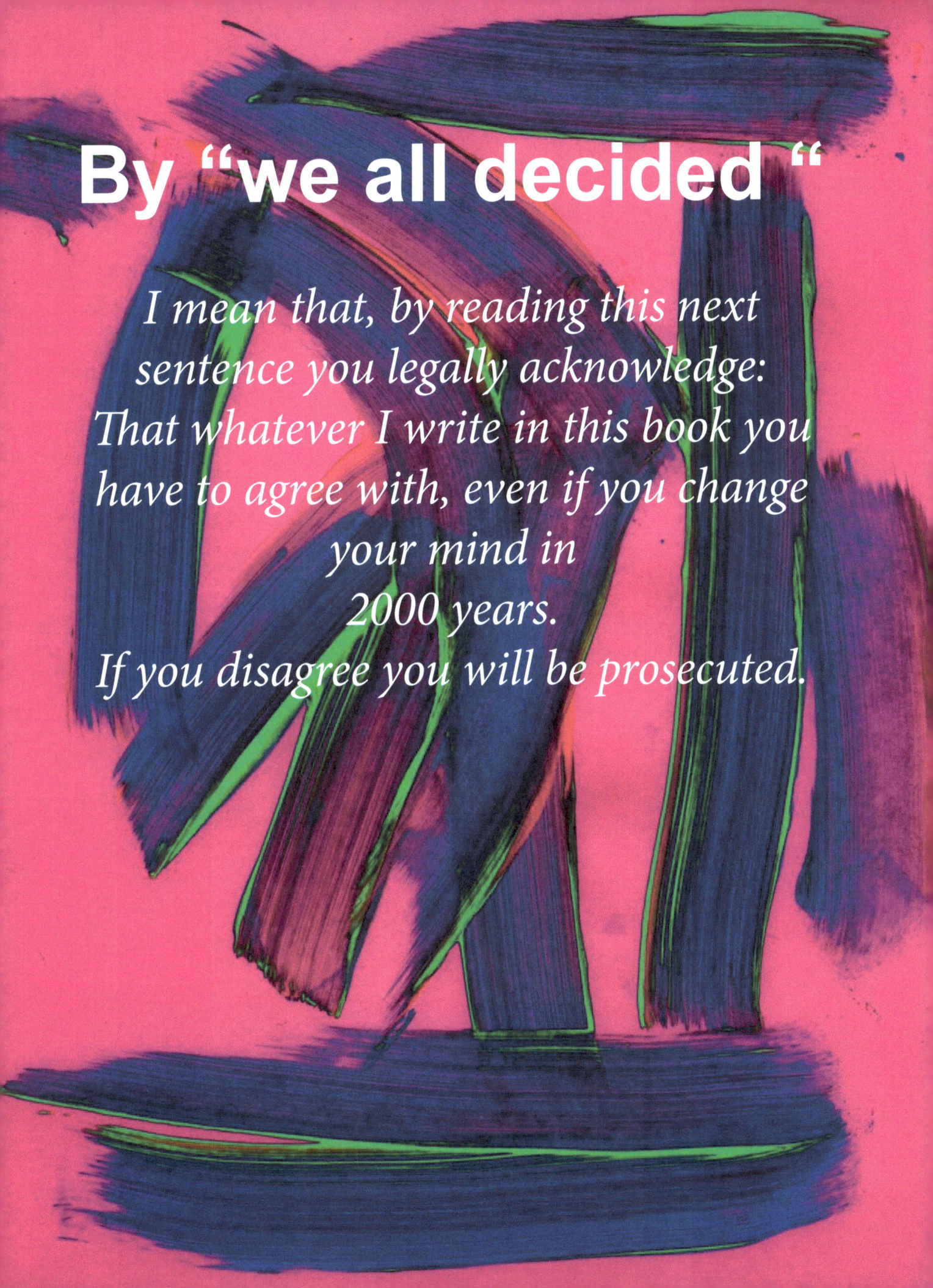

By "we all decided "

I mean that, by reading this next sentence you legally acknowledge: That whatever I write in this book you have to agree with, even if you change your mind in 2000 years. If you disagree you will be prosecuted.

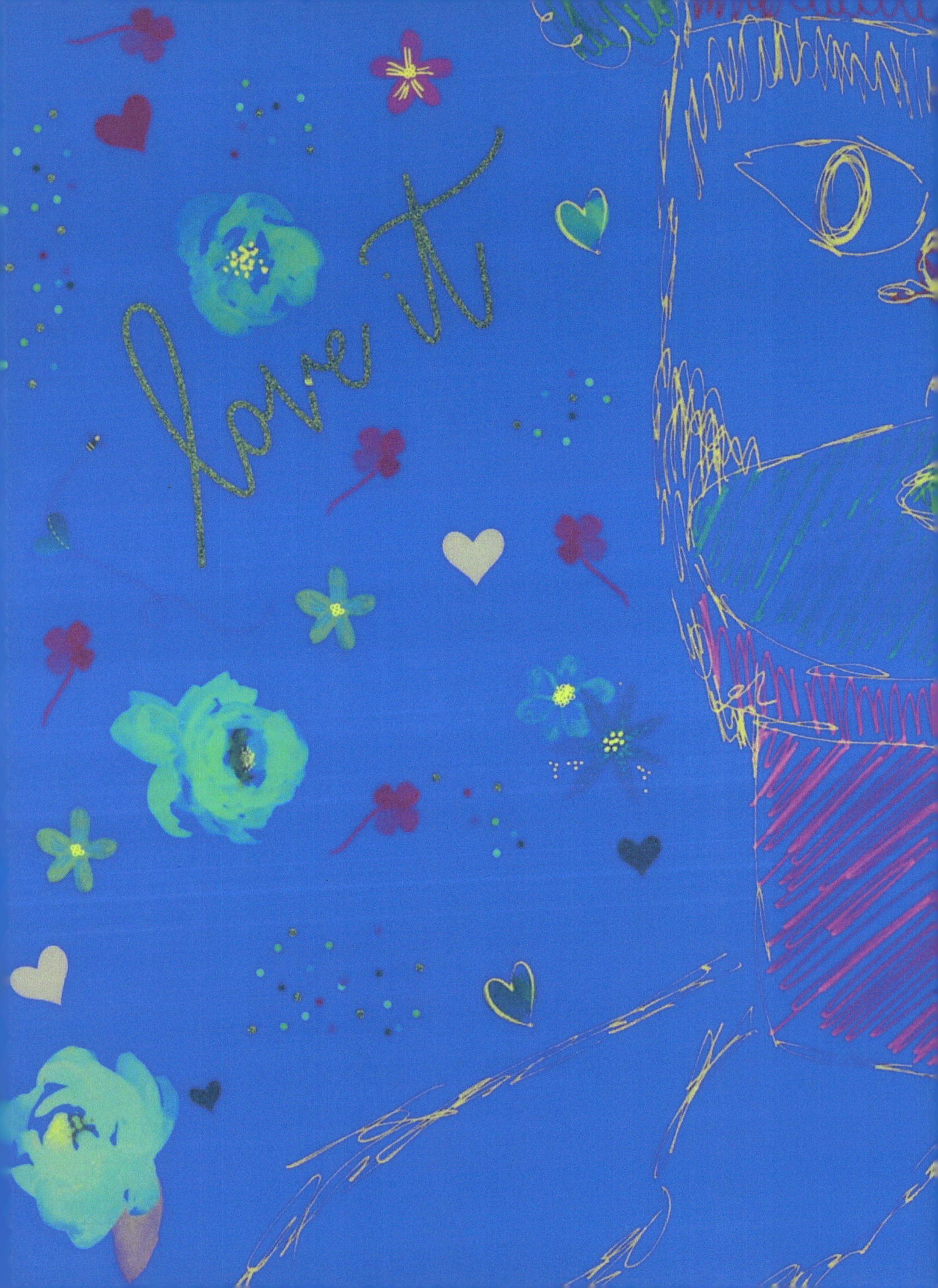

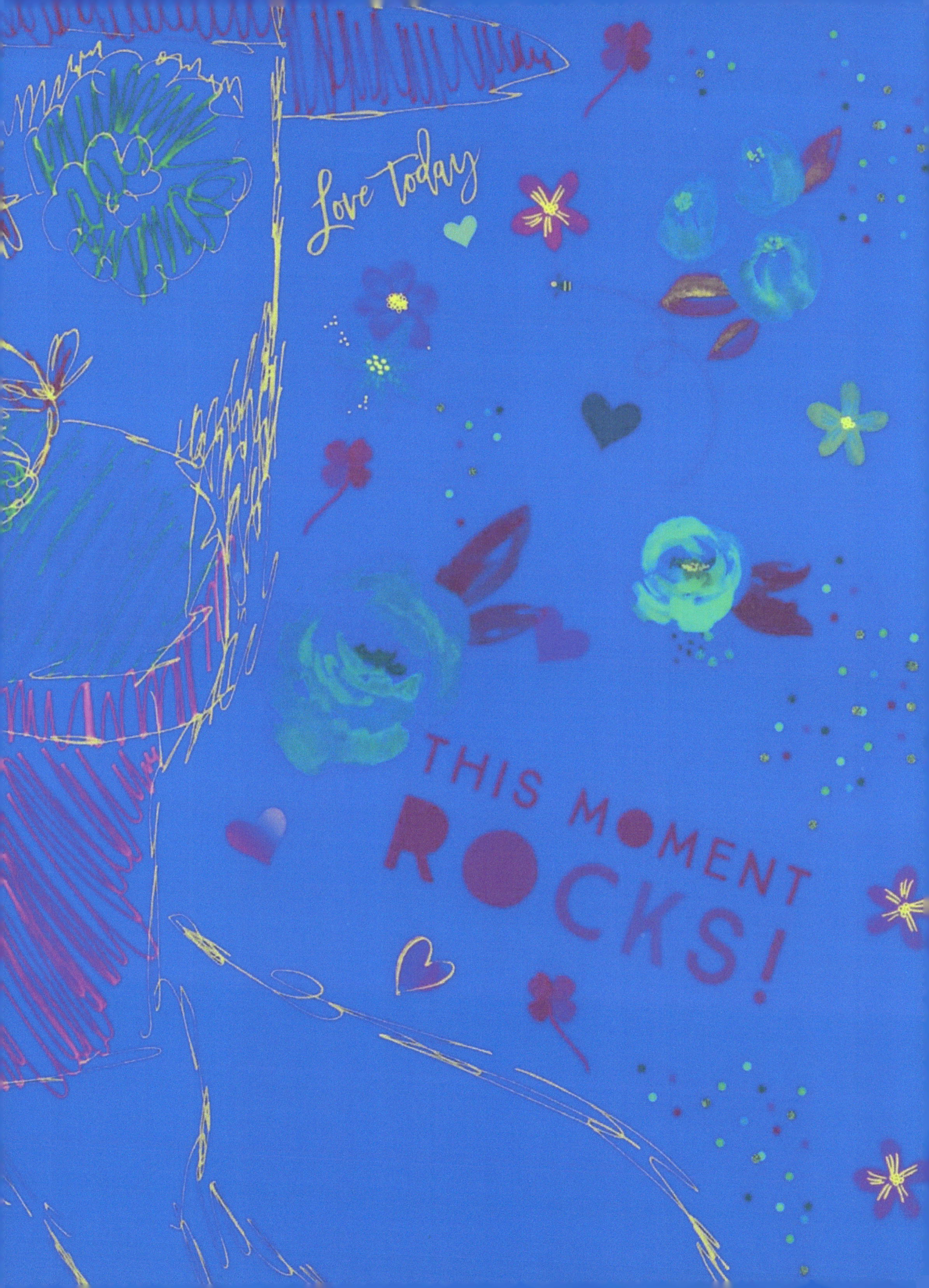

Ok so maybe Faith is a bit complicated, but it's also like, super cool.

Because if Juan wouldn't have been looking for Faith.

We wouldn't have this story.

So you could say that Faith brought us together.

Plus, thanks to Faith, Juan has that something.
Can Juan go back home now?

Because Juan is alone, don't you forget!

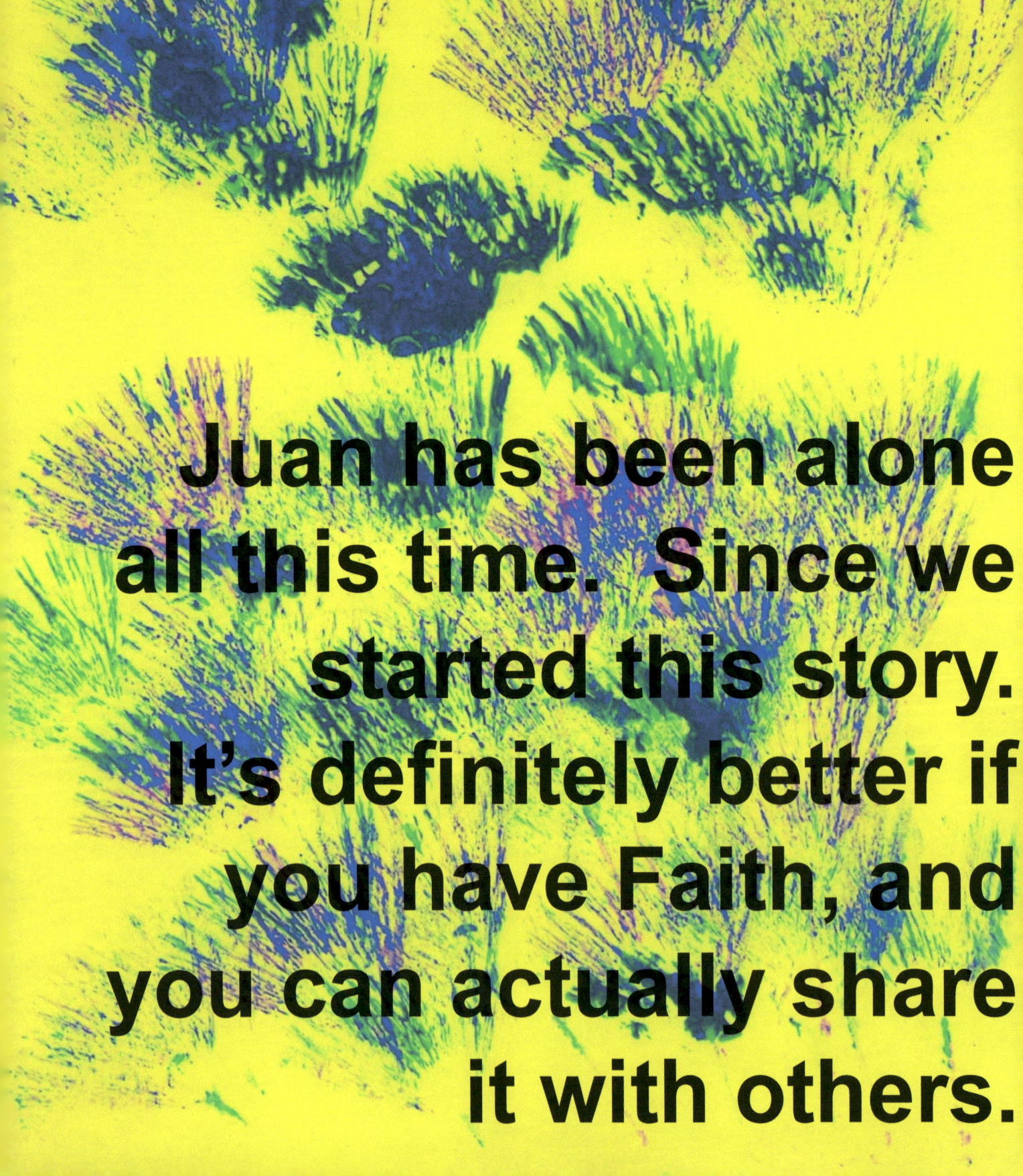

Wait!

If Juan has Faith and he is going back home...

It means this story is almost over!

Whaaaaaaat??? Nooooooooooo!!!

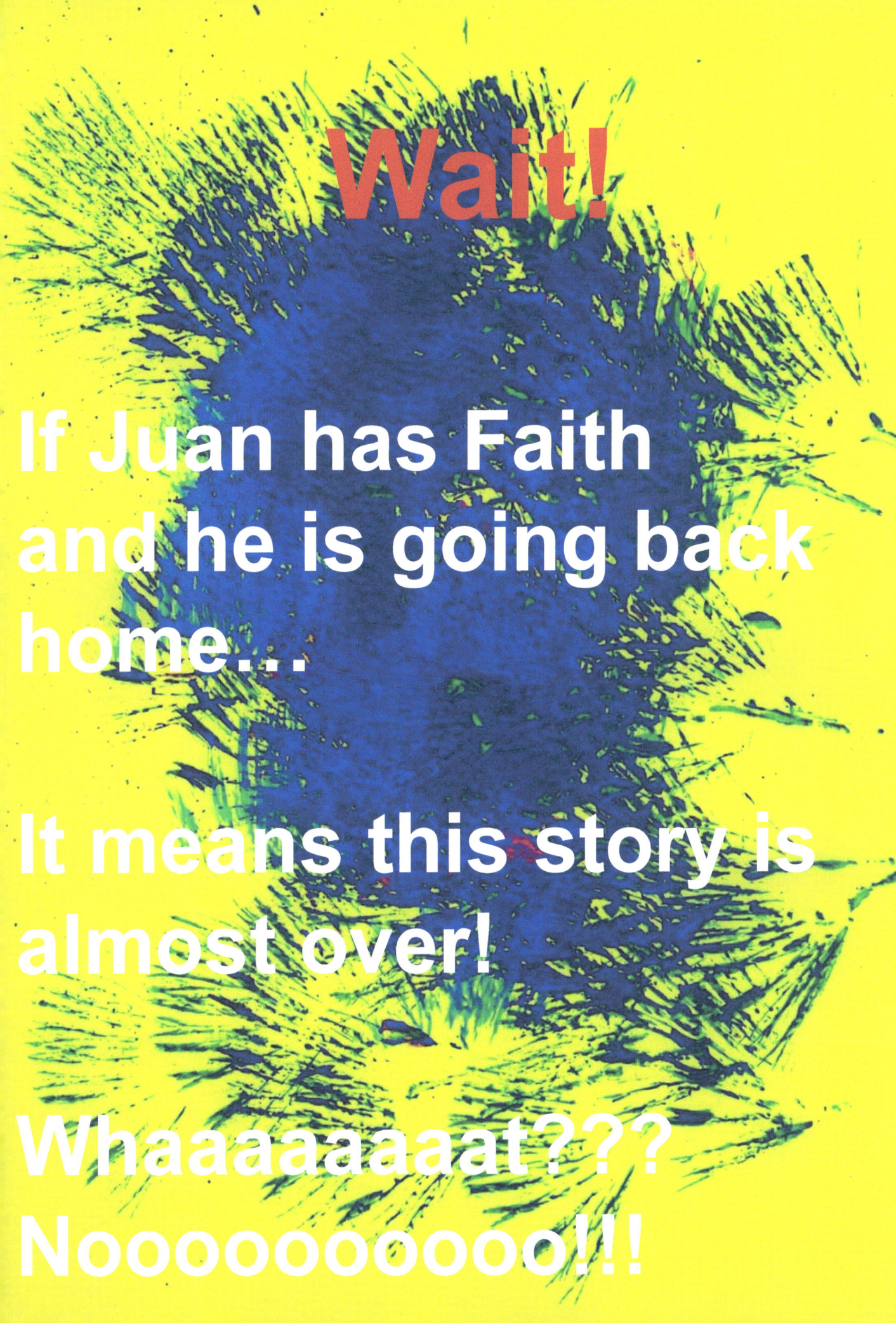

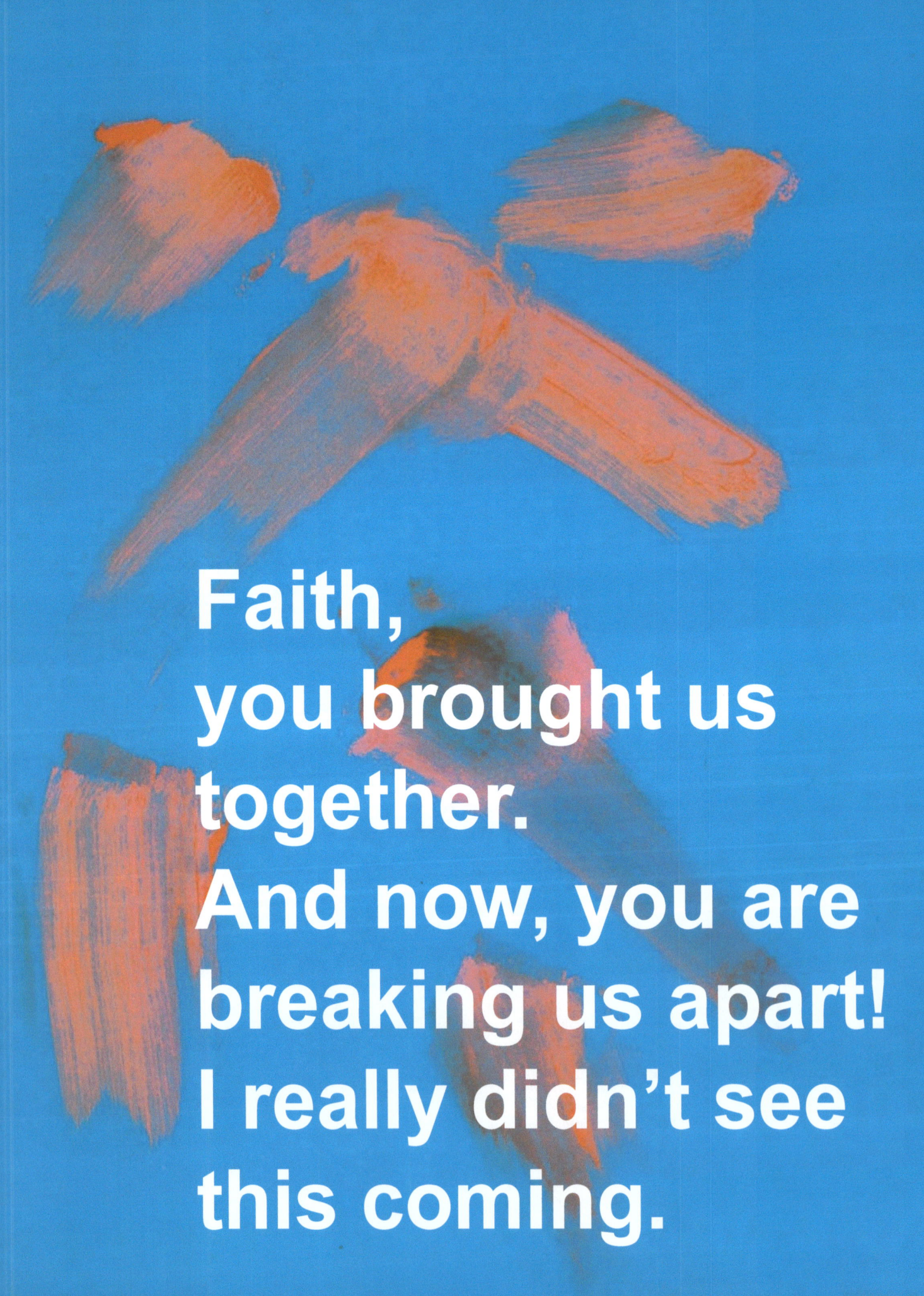

Why are you doing this to us? We were having so much fun because Juan was alone, don't you forget!

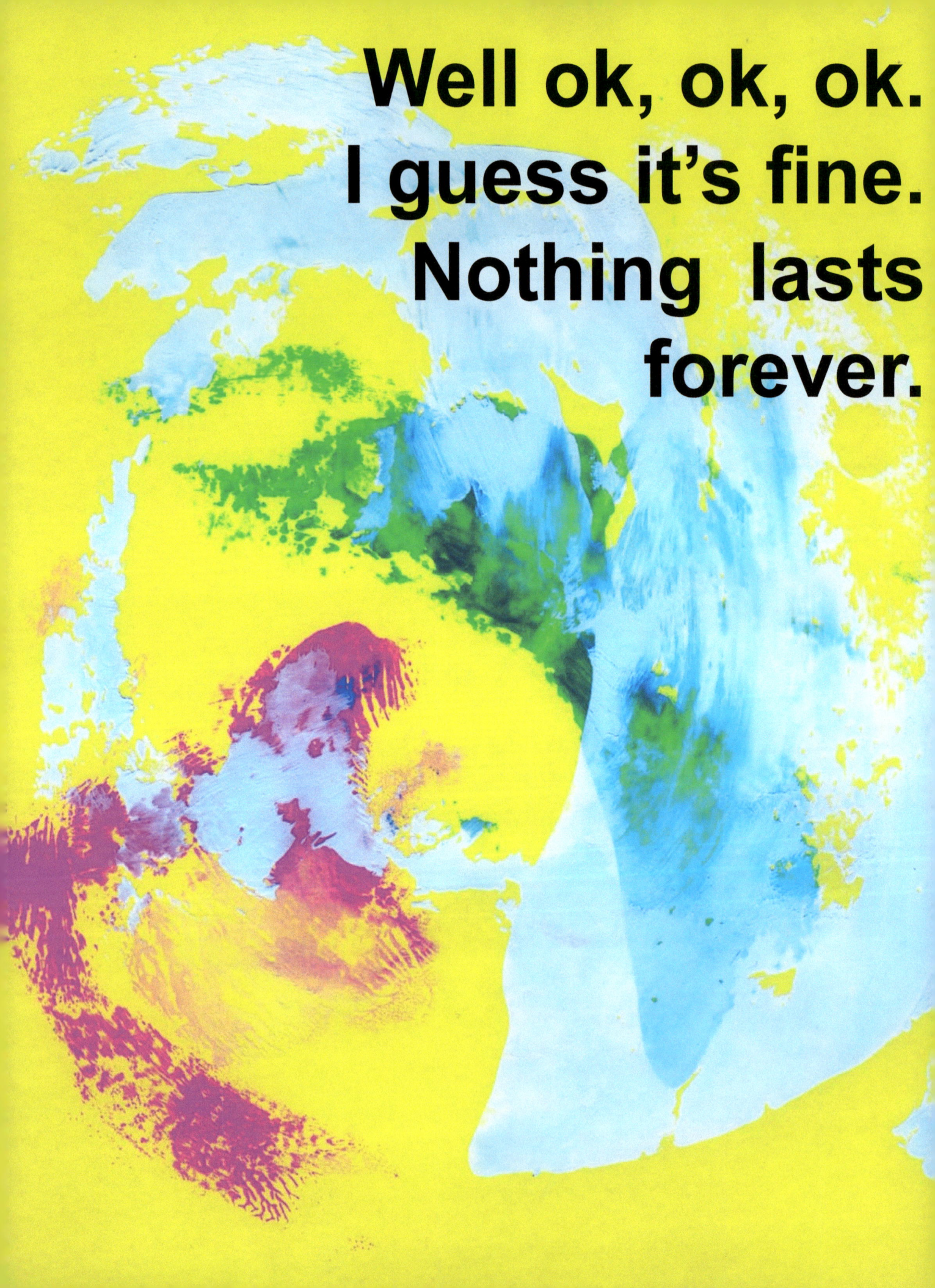

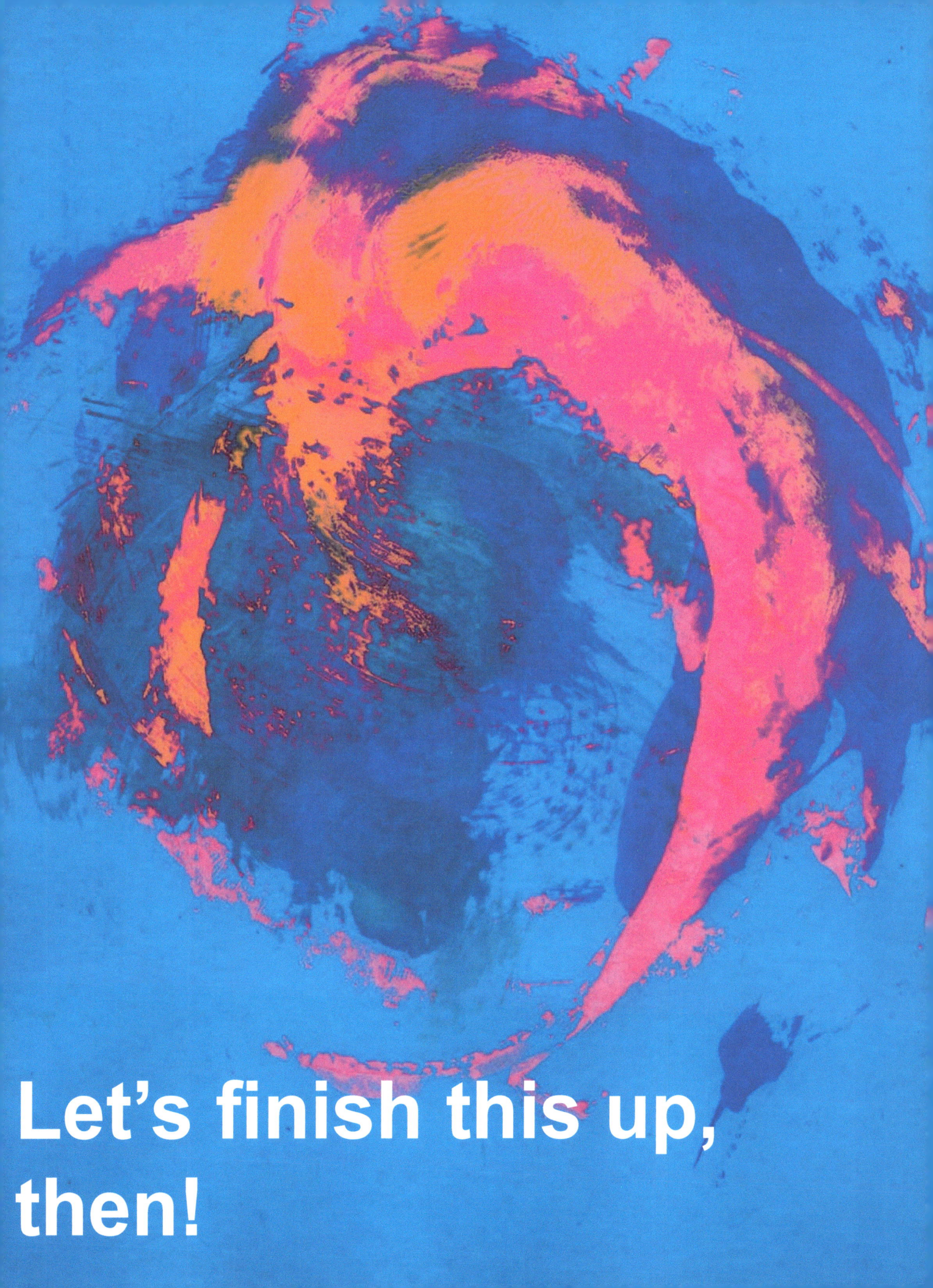

Don't forget how much fun we had along the way. And now we are totally friends. So it was totally worth it, but it's time for you to go to bed alone, Like Juan.

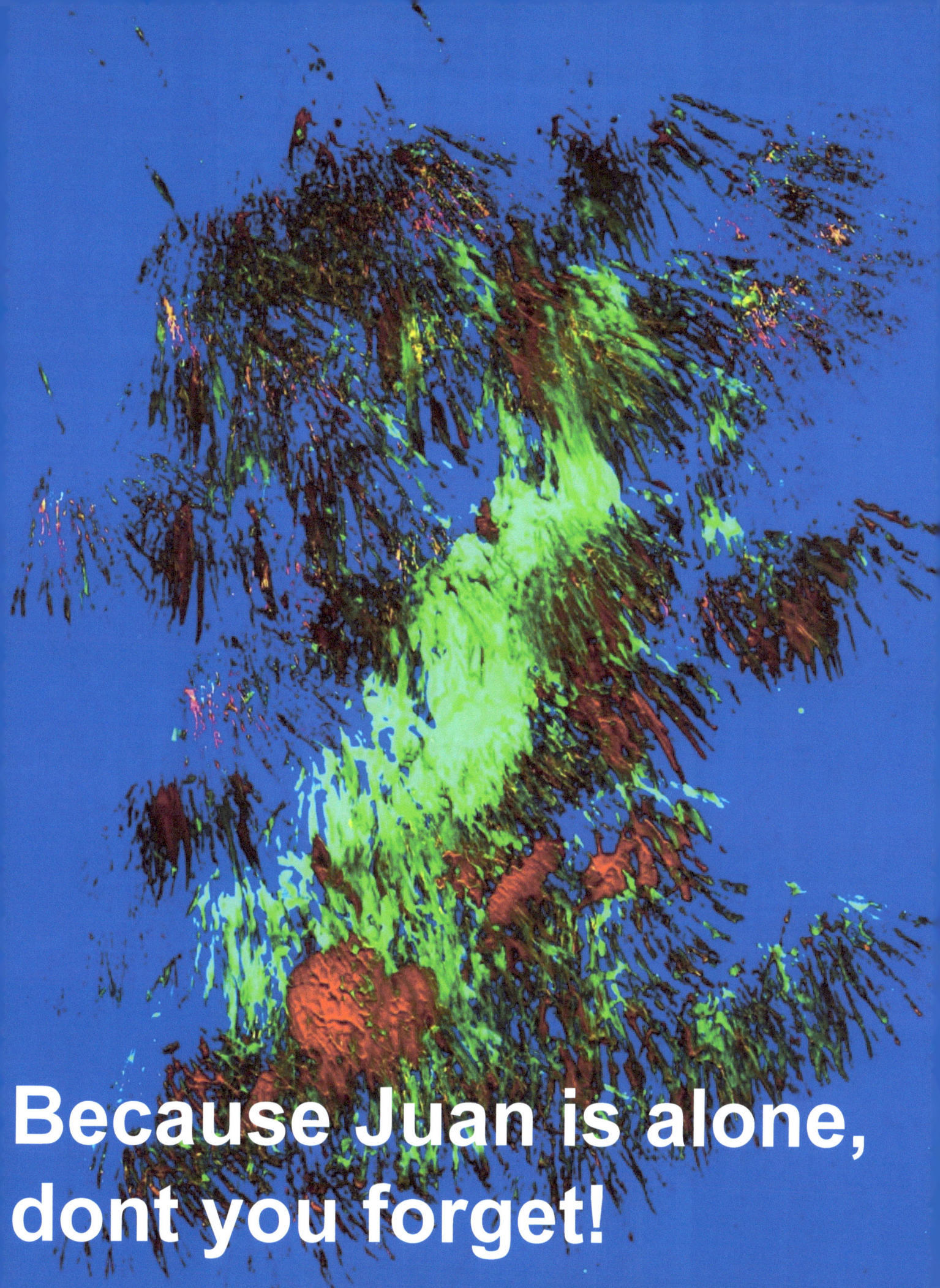

Remember how at the beginning of the story I said: "He's been known by many names. In this story his name is Juan."
Well it's because I am Juan, and I am writing this story.
And in my story, I write whatever I want.

Only by writing your own story, you can be your own hero. You can write whatever you want. However you want to write it.

But SHHH…

Don't tell anyone! It's a secret ☺

So if someday you are alone like me, and you get angry or scared.

Remember the Hope in your eyes.

Sooner, than later Hope will take you back home cause Hope is a badass.

And have Faith!

Faith should bring us together.

Don't let it divide us.

So with Hope in your eyes, and having Faith, you will make your way back home to the Earth and the Sun.

If you write your own story, of course.

And remember everything has to end, the good and the bad. No matter how dark it is, morning will come and it will be over.

Good thing we can always keep the memories of our journeys.

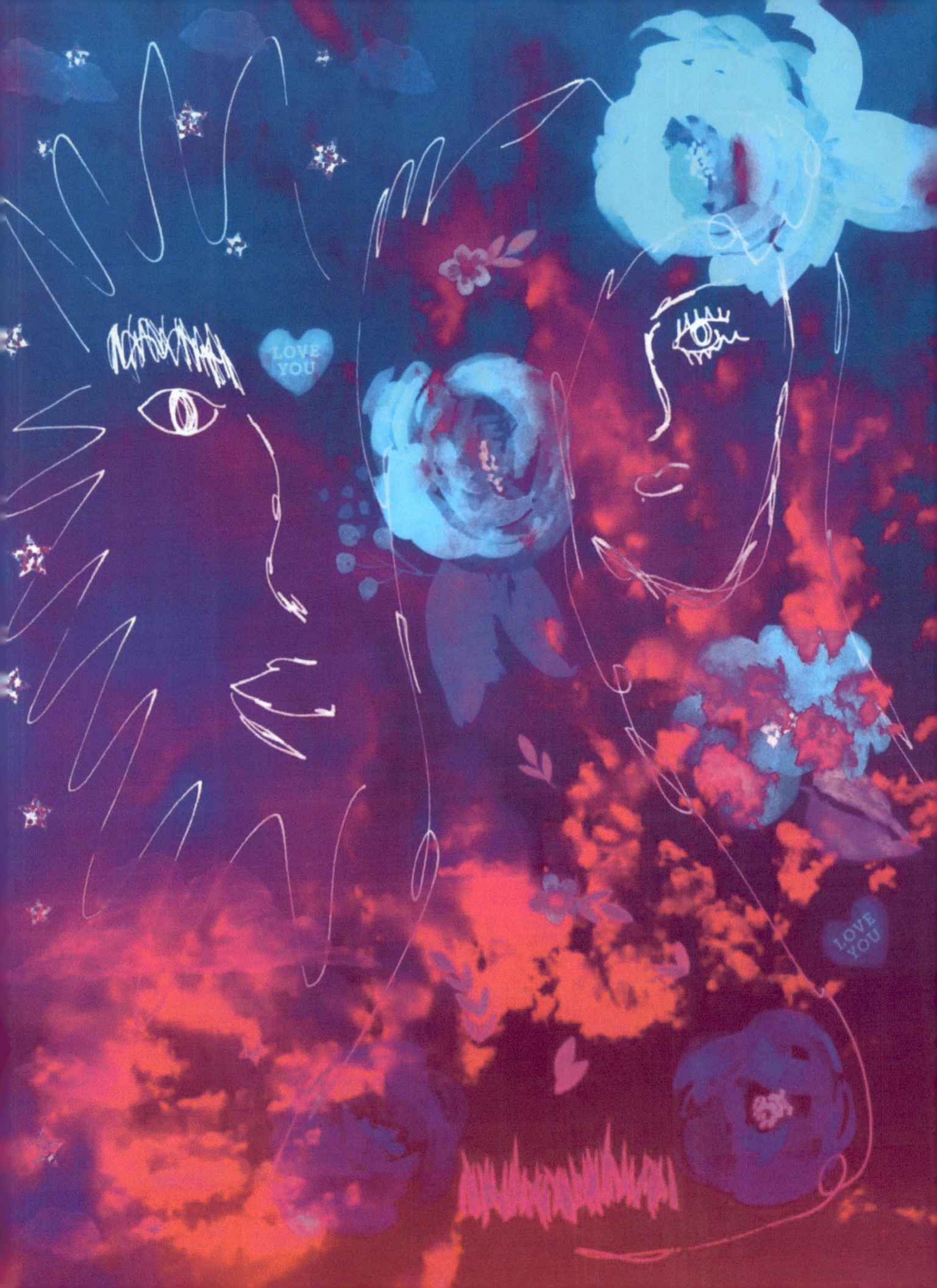

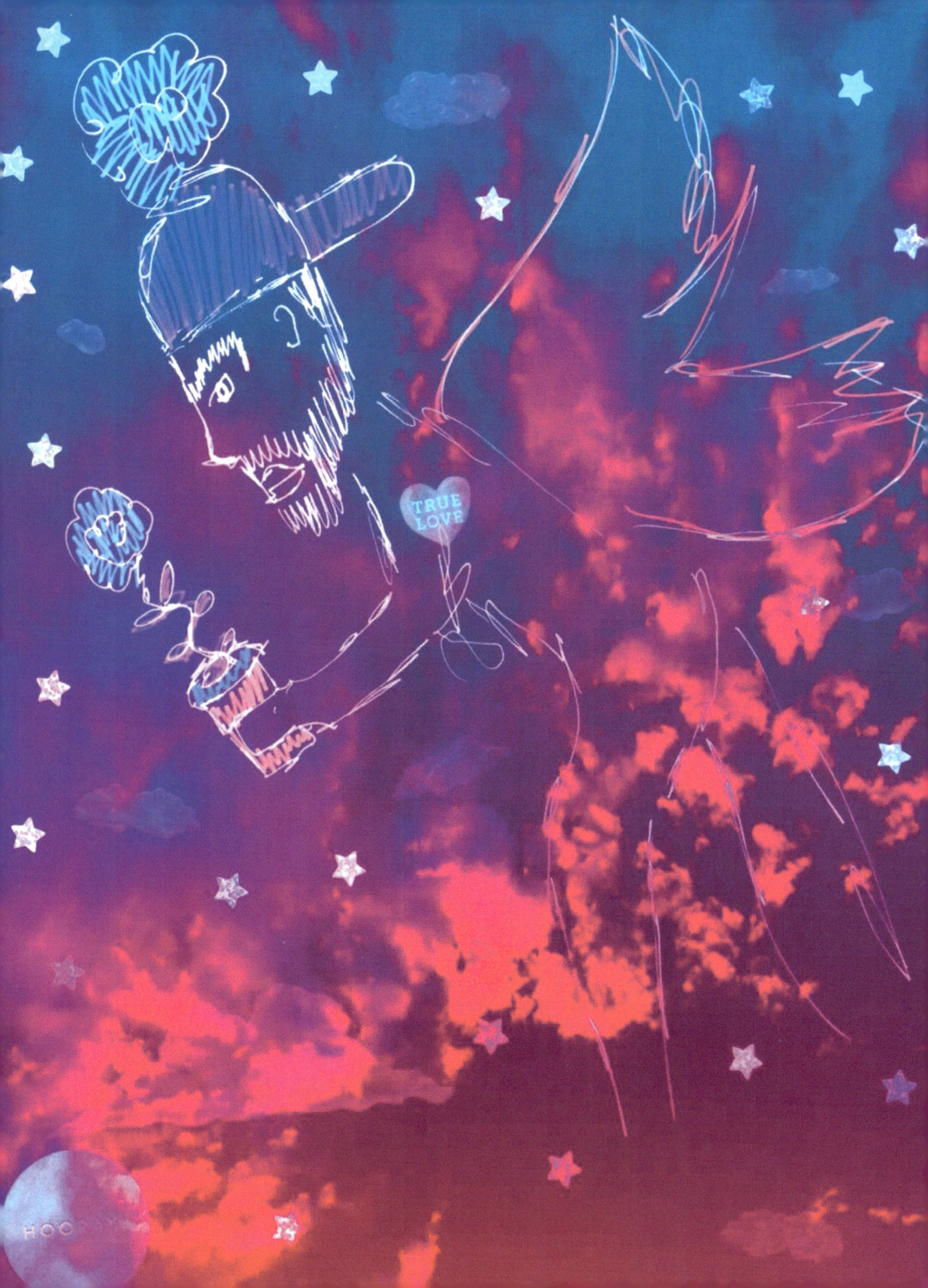

In this story I chose to be alone because I'm Juan, duh! What I am, no matter what it is, I choose.

In your life, you make your own decisions. You can be a frog, a doctor, an elephant, an astronaut, or a fart.

I chose to be alone because I can tell you stories.
I can, also, dance in my underwear if I want to.

The only problem is that if I'm not alone, then I'm not Juan.

Because Juan is alone, don't you forget!

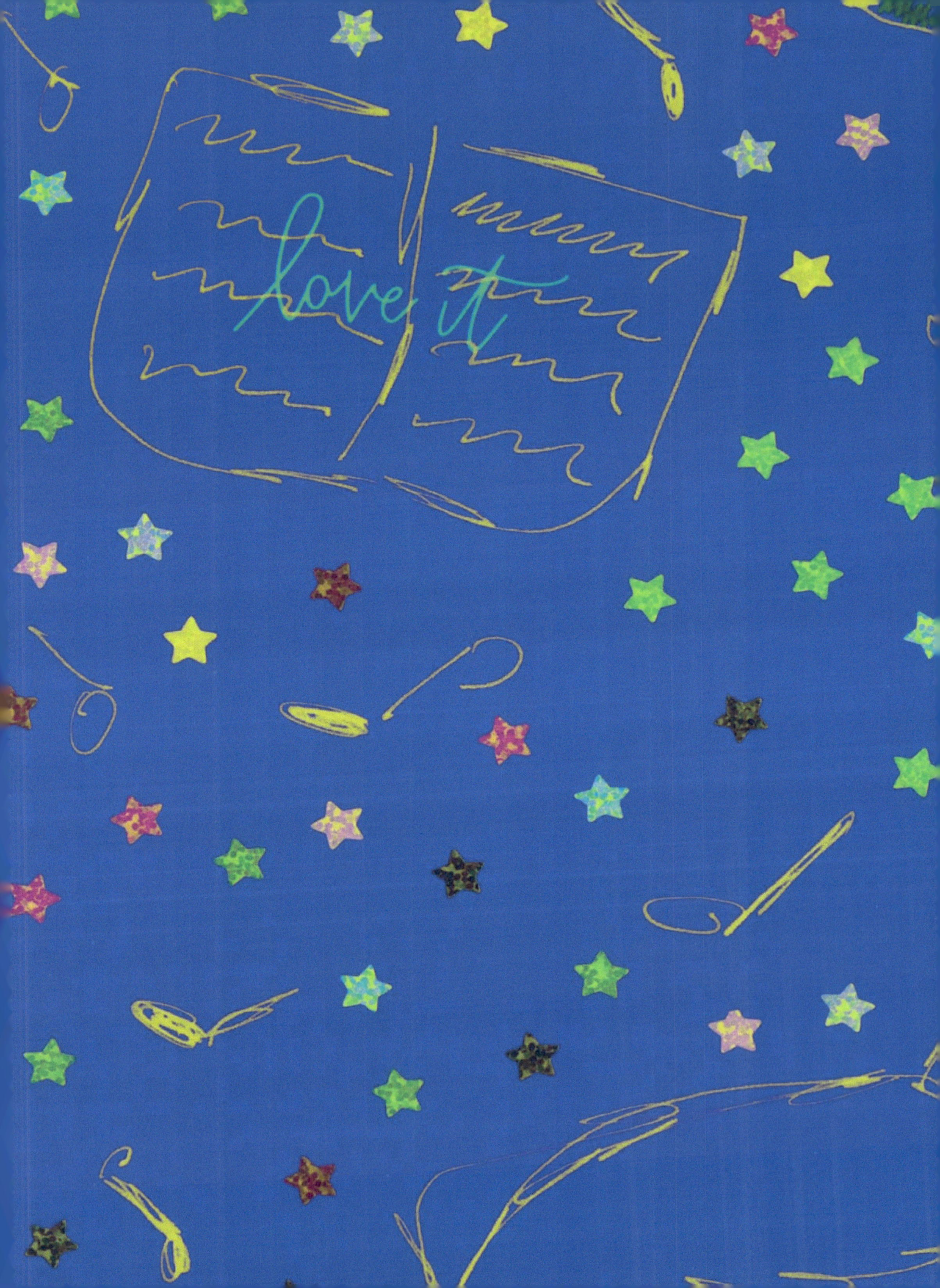

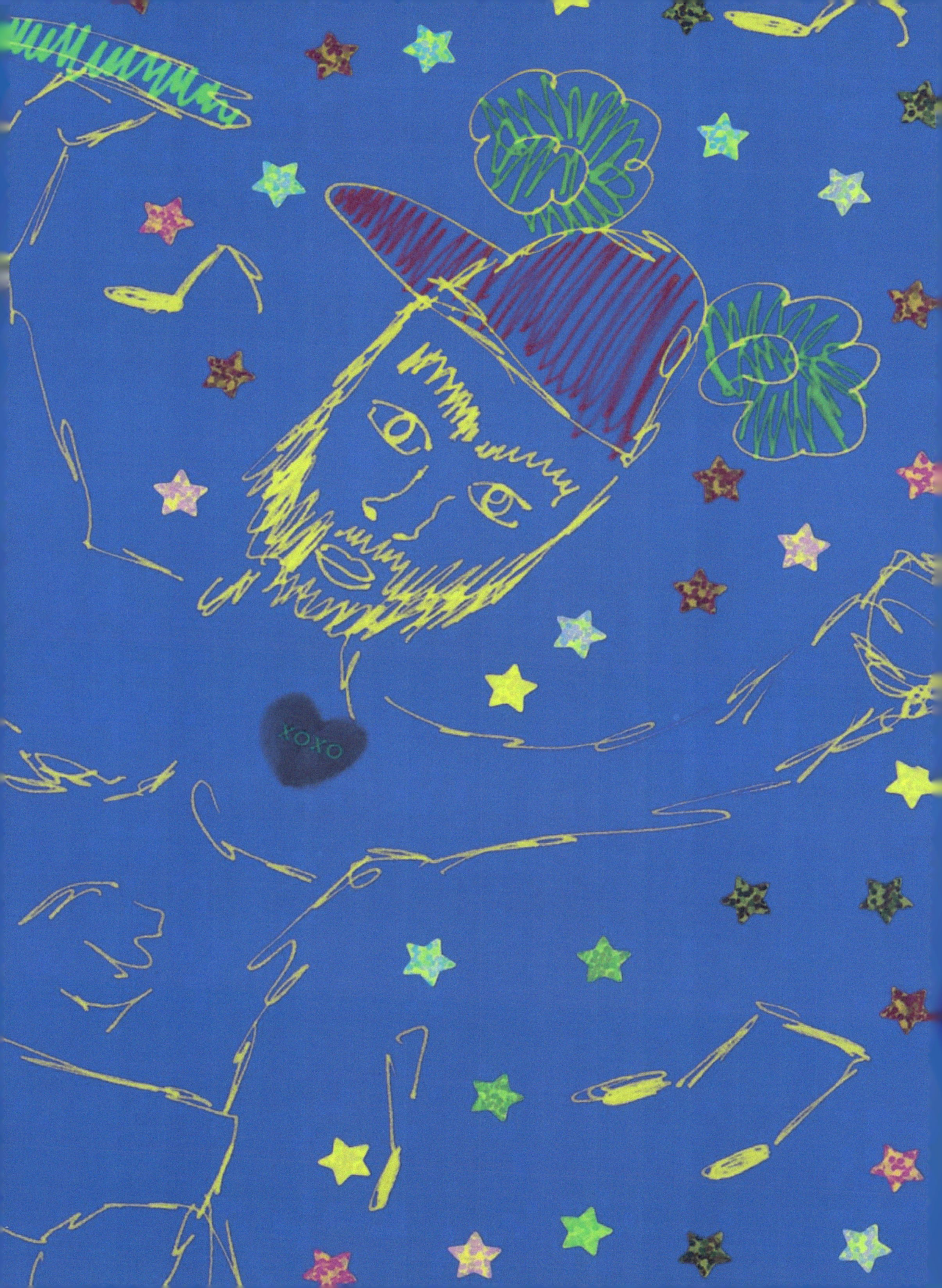

Oops! My mom just walked into my room. So I'm not alone anymore.

So I'm not Juan.

Since I'm not Juan. I didn't write this story.

So this story doesn't exist.

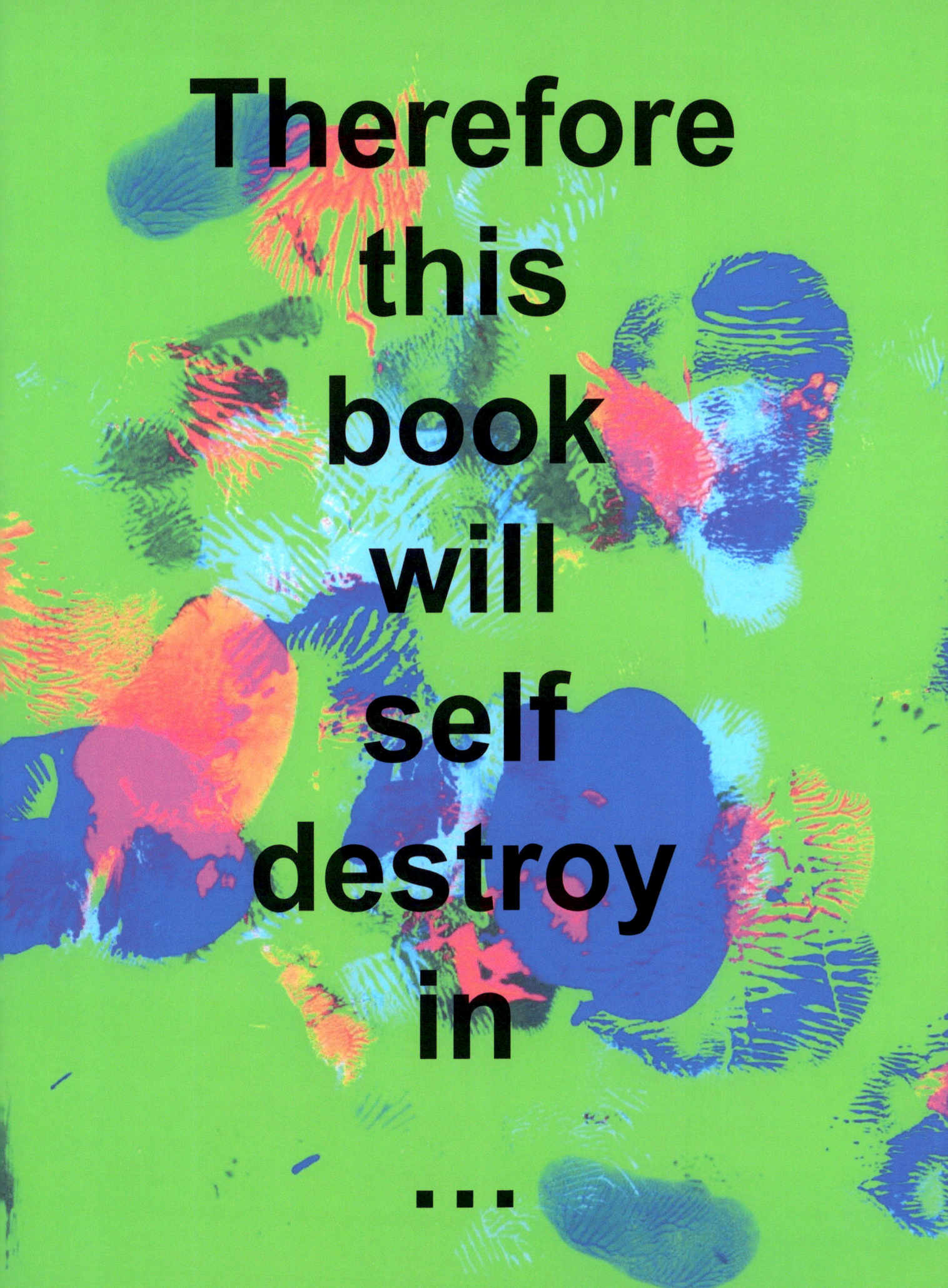

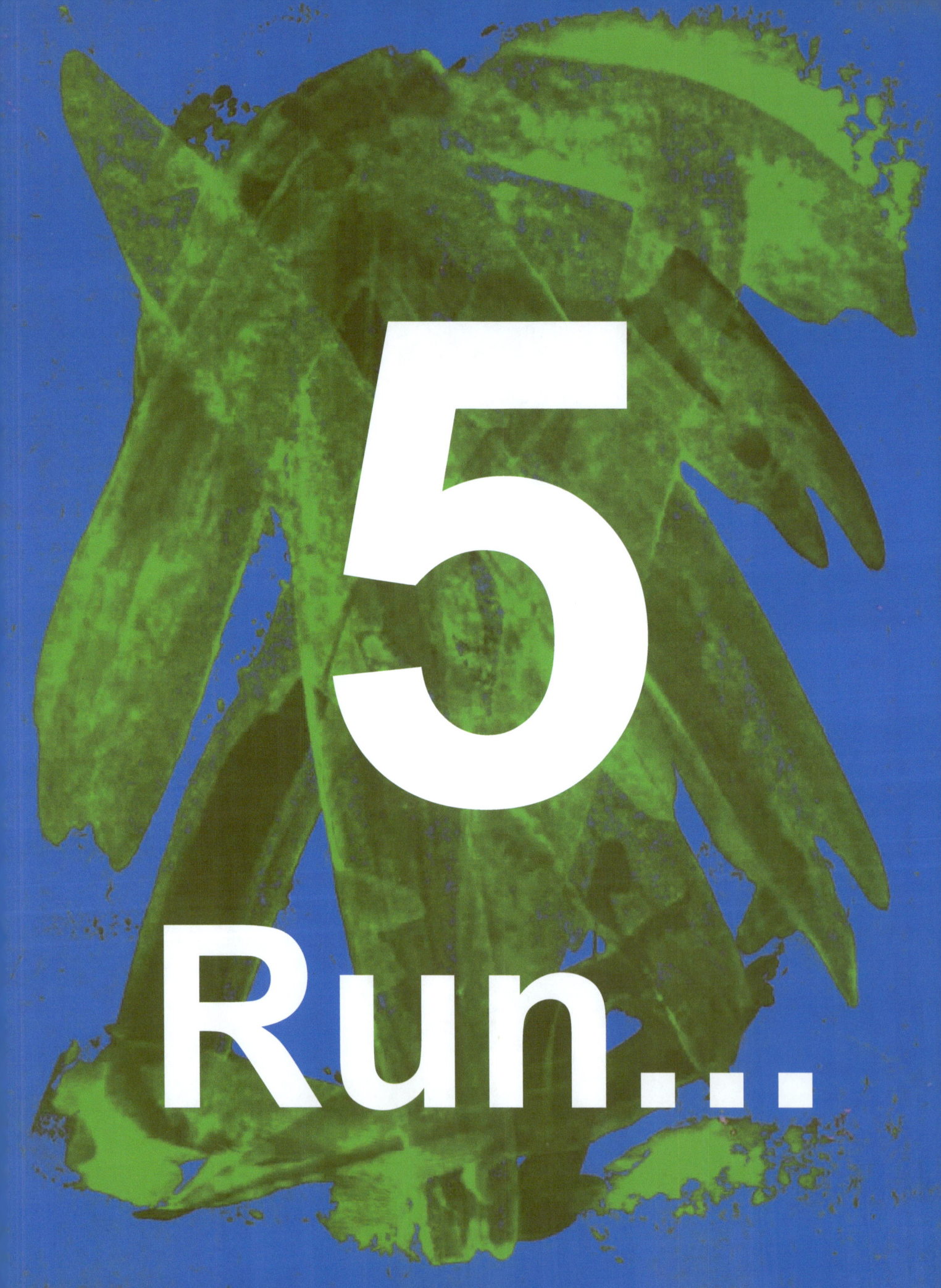

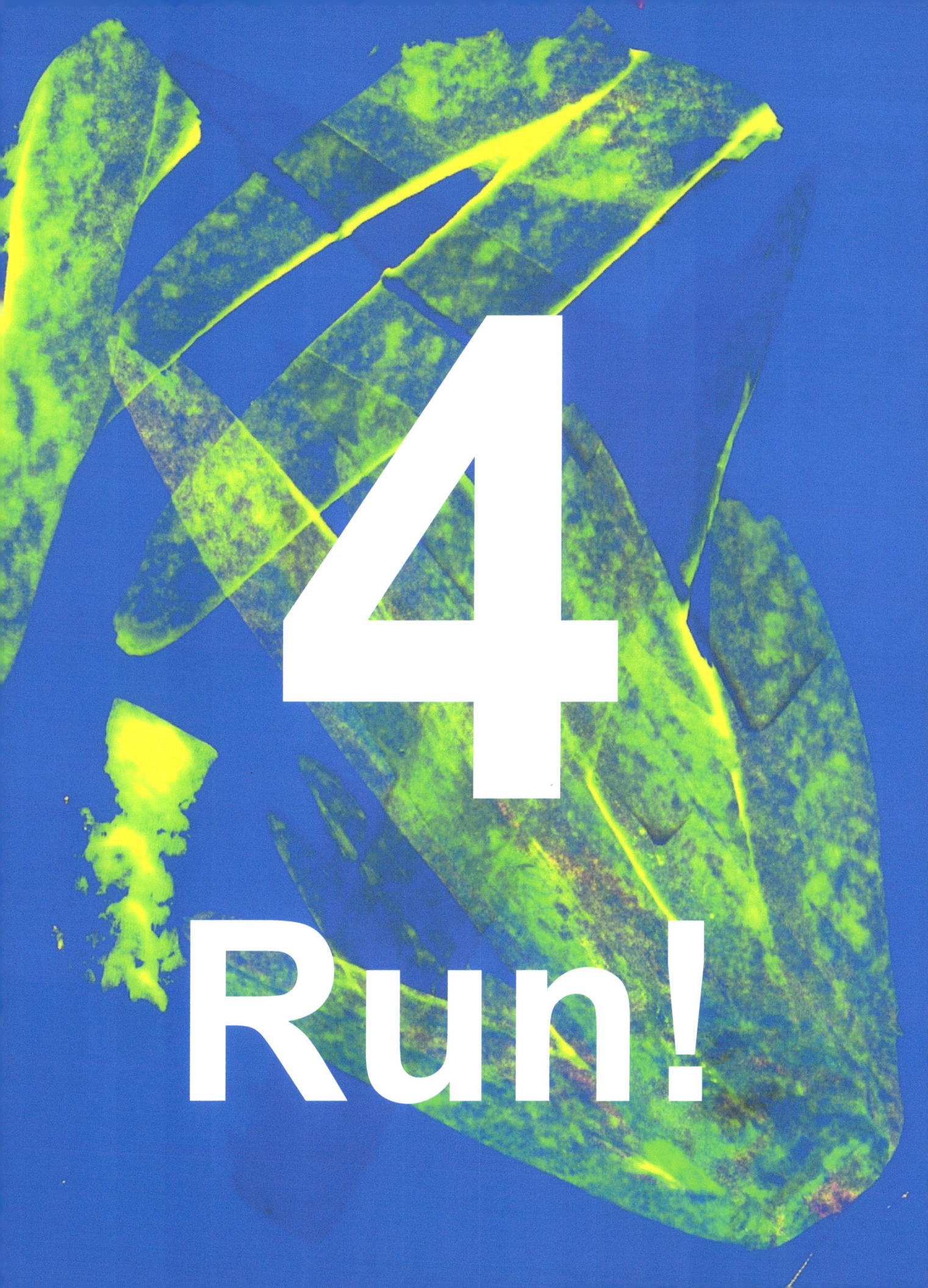

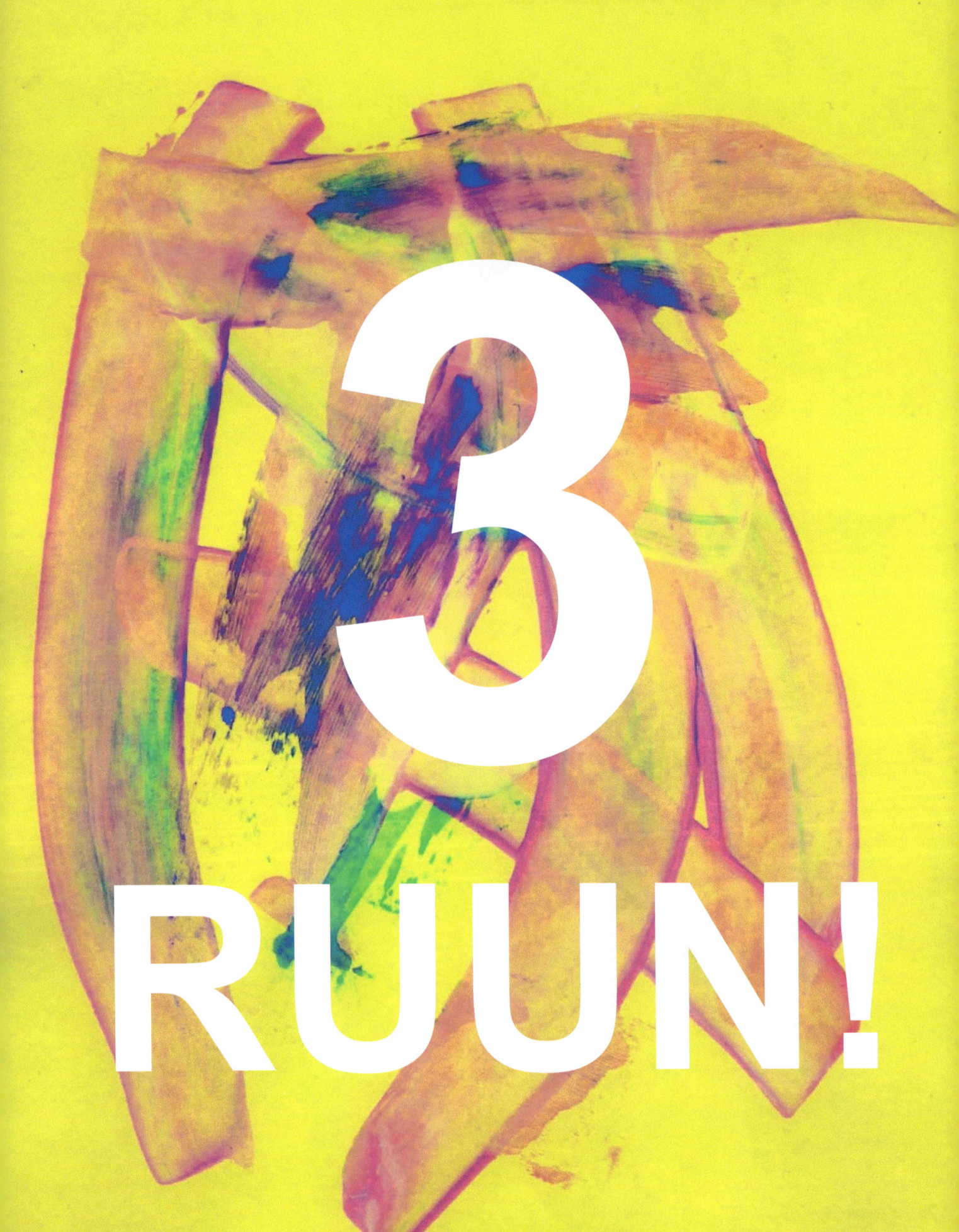

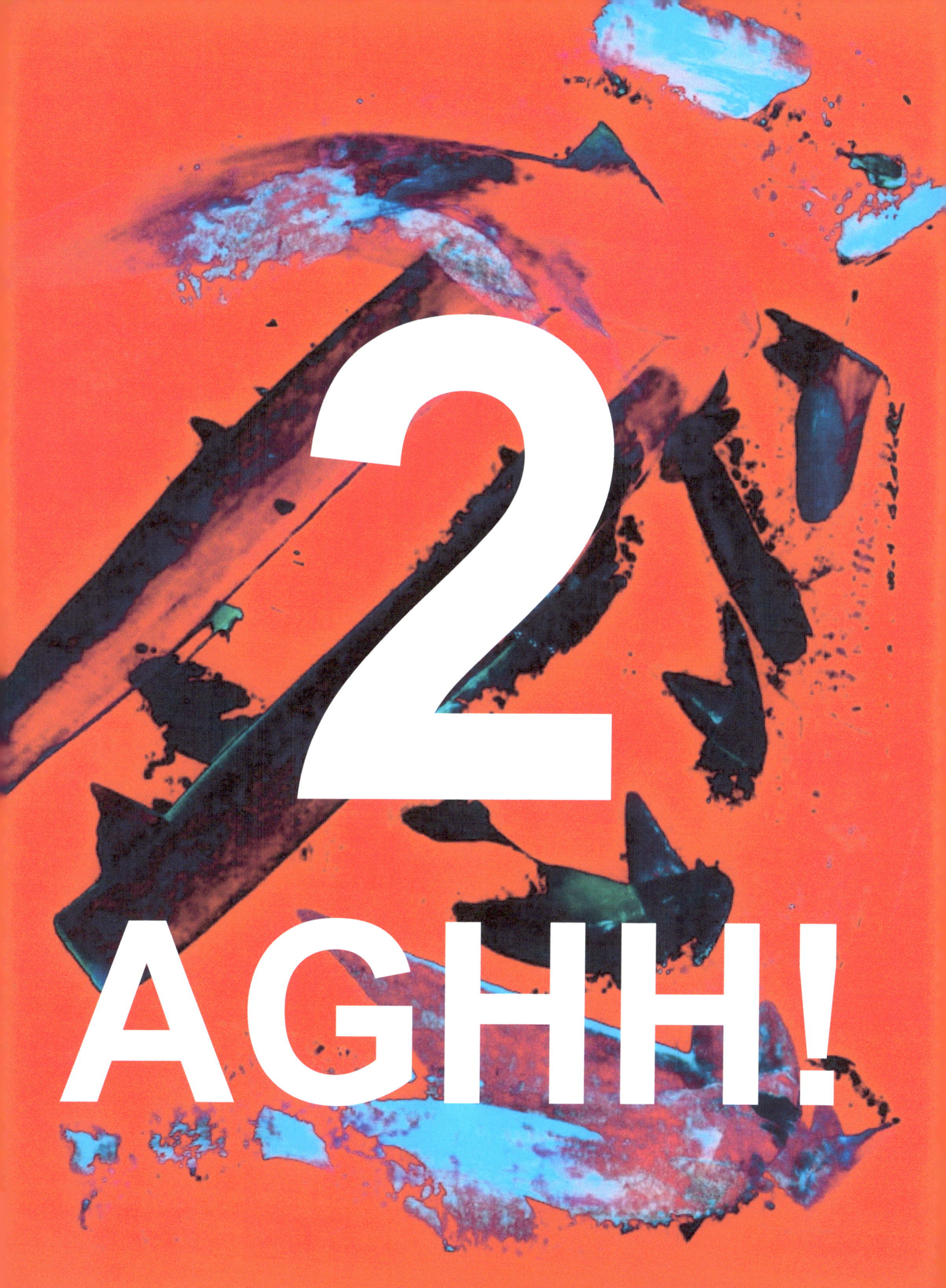

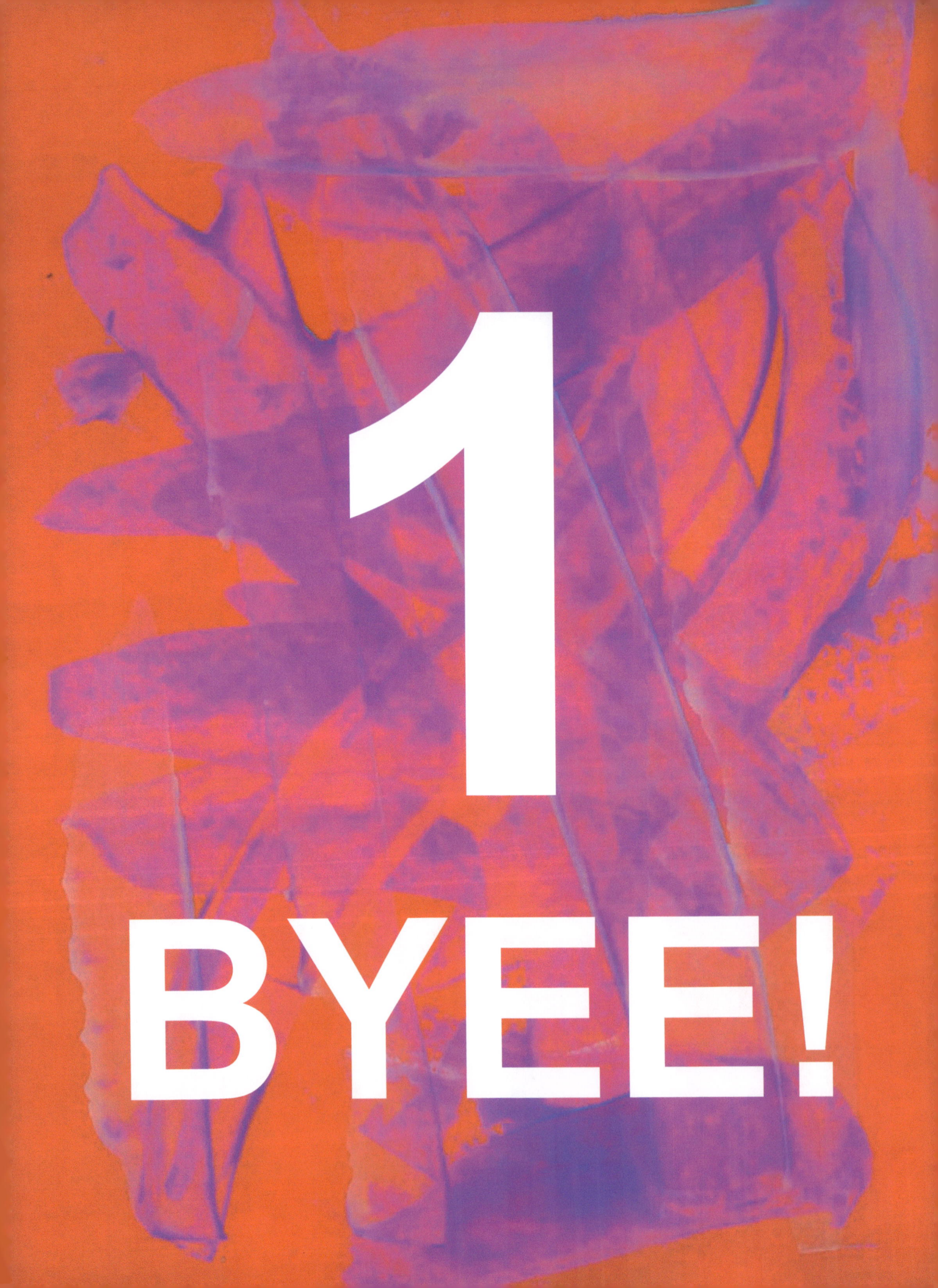

Kabooooooom
chacalhglb rkdfbllrnf;; gnlrebf.fgh

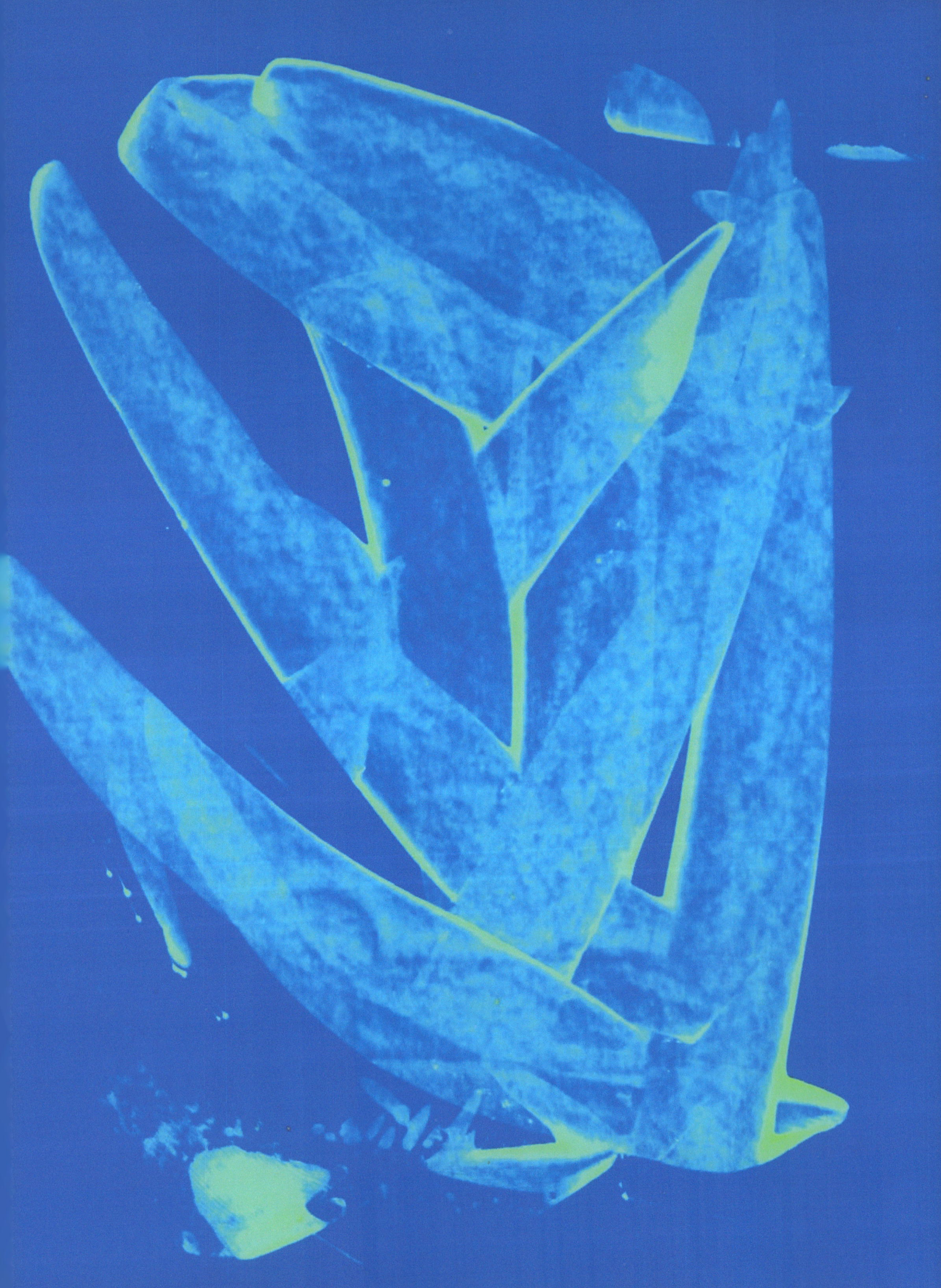

I don't know your name, nor I care. You are my friend anyways, duh! We went through this story together.

I love you!

Ok, bye ☺
Juan or not…